A Field Guide to Custer's Camps

A Field Guide to Custer's Camps

On the March to the Little Bighorn

by Don Weinell

Heritage Guide Series Volume 2

Thomas D. Isern, Editor

Fargo, North Dakota

NDSU NORTH DAKOTA STATE
UNIVERSITY PRESS

Dept. 2360, P.O. Box 6050, Fargo, ND 58108-6050
www.ndsupress.org

A Field Guide to Custer's Camps: On the March to the Little Bighorn
By Don Weinell

Copyright © 2021 by North Dakota State University Press
First Edition

ISBN: 978-1-946163-27-1
LCCN: 2021939692

Cover and interior design by Deb Tanner
Photographs (unless otherwise indicated) by Don Weinell
Nataly Routledge, Editorial Intern
Zachary Vietz, Oliver West Sime, Graduate Assistants in Publishing & Publicity

Cover photo by Don Weinell

The publication of *A Field Guide to Custer's Camps: On the March to the Little Bighorn* is made possible by the support of donors to the NDSU Press Fund and the NDSU Press Endowment Fund.

For copyright permissions, please contact Suzanne Kelley at 701-231-6848 or suzanne.kelley@ndsu.edu.

Printed in the United States of America

Publisher's Cataloging-in-Publication Data is available from the Library of Congress

This book is dedicated to the thousands of reenactors, worldwide, who keep history alive for the rest of us.

Contents

List of Figures

Foreword by the Series Editor

Flip forward with me to page sixteen and we join our author, Don Weinell, at Custer Camp #3, just southwest of New Salem, North Dakota. You'll find the campsite is easily accessible, with a pretty good section road running alongside. And over there, a mile north, rises School Hill, where Salem Sue, the world's largest Holstein, overlooks Interstate 94. You'll have to have a look at her, too, right? Go ahead, get off the subject and lose yourself, or find yourself.

The Heritage Guide Series of North Dakota State University Press exists for the orientation and edification of independent travelers experiencing the heritage resources of the northern plains. All you FITs (free independent travelers) out there, Weinell is one of you. Experiencing the Great Plains landscape and finding things in it are what you are about. *A Field Guide to Custer's Camps* has a place in your vehicle, whether two-wheeled or four-.

Yes, we know . . . Custer . . . and here is yet another book about him. If you picked this one up, then there is a good chance you are a Custer buff. It's possible that Colonel W. A. Graham's *The Custer Myth* (1953) is Holy Writ in your house. If that is the case, then Weinell is your dragoman (go ahead and web-search that—if you're a FIT, you love to look things up) for a prairie pilgrimage.

If you are not a Custer buff or a bicyclist, and you are attracted to the work for some other wonky reason, here is our apologia for another book about one of the most belabored figures in American history. It is a work of exploration. When Custer crossed the plains for the last time in 1876, he had some idea where he was going—Major General Alfred Sully had gone before him in 1864—but even with the counsel of his scouts, Custer was feeling his way through a difficult land possessed by combative people, by a savvy akicita defending a beloved makoche. Tracking him, pausing where he pitched a tent, getting a little lost now and then, you experience the land as he did. It was Custer, after all, who exhorted us to quit calling our prairies "the Great American Desert" and to refer to them instead as "the Great Plains."

Moreover, as you pause, you reflect on decisions taken, choices made—command decisions, reasoned choices. You are moved to practice what military historians call "inherent military probability," reverse-engineering a narrative of what happened in 1876 by asking yourself, what would, or did, a trained officer do under these circumstances, in this place? Prepare to be fascinated. If you have the chops in military science, you can practice your military terrain analysis (KOCOA, anyone?) here, too.

Now, recognize you are shadowboxing with history. The conflict of 1876 was an episode in an asymmetrical war, militarily and historically. By which I mean, the sources, too—I say with apologies to Col. Graham—are asymmetrical. James Welch effectively reminded us in 1994 with *Killing Custer* that we are arrogant and ignorant if we rely on military reports and disregard Indigenous sources as to what went down in 1876, or at any point in the long history of Indian-white contact and conflict on the plains. Still and all, the white guys wrote more stuff down. This makes it all the more interesting and necessary to use the imagination, exercising inherent military probability, to reconstruct the thinking and action of Indigenous defenders of the land. This is a whole additional layer to enrich your experience of every site named in this book.

So get out there and look, and think. This book will take you places. It is, as our author says, "an excuse for even greater adventures."

Thomas D. Isern
Editor, Heritage Guide Series
Professor of History and University Distinguished Professor
North Dakota State University

Preface

In the summer of 2018, a friend and I bicycled from Fort Abraham Lincoln near Bismarck, North Dakota, to the Little Bighorn Battlefield National Monument near Crow Agency, Montana. We wanted to follow, as closely as possible, the route taken by General George Armstrong Custer in 1876 as he marched west toward his disastrous encounter with the Sioux and Northern Cheyenne. Both of us were experienced bicycle tourists, he more so than I, but I was the navigator on the journey.

Travelers by bicycle tend to fall into one of two groups. Some like to begin a trip with only a general idea of where they will be riding. Others, like me, prefer to plan out every possible detail of the trip in advance. In fact, I have been accused of enjoying the planning more than the actual riding. I confess there is some truth to this. I can easily spend hours looking over maps and dreaming of the adventures to be found along all those squiggly lines.

When attempting to follow a route already traveled by others, planning becomes paramount. Early into the process, however, I discovered that very little information regarding Custer's trail was available. The information existed, but it was not compiled in such a way that modern travelers could easily decipher. With this book I hope to correct that.

The sad reality is that only sparse evidence of Custer's actual trail remains. Wagon ruts and hoof prints visible well into the 1930s have long since disappeared under the plow or as the result of natural erosion. Away from the interstates and highways, though, the landscape today looks very much as it did when the 7th Cavalry crossed it almost 150 years ago. You, the modern traveler, can still enjoy many of the sights, sounds, and smells that Custer's troops experienced on their journey. And, unless you are hiking or cycling the route, you can experience it in much greater comfort.

Even though most of the trail is not visible, you can get a close approximation of the route by visiting each of the sites Custer's men camped at along the way. Between May 17, 1876, and June 24, 1876, twenty-seven campsites were established. Today, most are on private land but are easily seen from public roadways. Keep in mind, however, that the term "road" in North Dakota and Montana does not necessarily have the same meaning as it does in more populated states. Many are unpaved; some are barely passable following the slightest amount of rain. If you get stuck, it might be a long walk to any assistance. Plan accordingly.

It was late June and early July when we bicycled the route; a little later in the year than when Custer traveled it. We did not have any snow, but 2018 was an exceptionally wet year. Prairies and fields that normally would have been dry and brown were green. Everyone we spoke with told us how unusually lush the vegetation was. Wildflowers flourished. Streams that may be crossable in a normal year were still swollen. Thunderstorms were an almost daily occurrence. While camping near the mouth of Rosebud Creek in Montana, we were struck by a severe storm that packed fifty-mile-per-hour winds and covered the ground with hail. Many of the diaries of the soldiers told similar tales.

As you follow the route, I encourage you to stop and visit the towns you pass through along the way. Most did not exist in Custer's day, but each has a unique history worth exploring. Talk to the residents. They have their own stories to share. At a slower pace, cyclists can see and experience the more subtle nuances of their surroundings. In a car at highway speeds, you must make a conscious decision to slow down and soak it all in. The effort is worth it. Use the 7th Cavalry's path through North Dakota and Montana as we did: as an excuse for even greater adventures.

Figure 1. The author and his trusty steed at the Little Bighorn Battlefield National Monument. Photo courtesy Kevin Nee.

Introduction

Nearly three hundred thousand people visit the Little Bighorn Battlefield National Monument each year, but just seeing the battlefield is like watching only the last fifteen minutes of a movie or reading the final few pages of a novel: the context is lost. Even the greatest battles taken out of context teach us little. Historians need a wide view of the events leading up to a conflict if they are to fully appreciate its final moments. The Battle of the Little Bighorn only concluded in Montana; it began almost six weeks earlier and over four hundred miles away on the banks of the Missouri River in North Dakota. If you wish to understand Custer's ending, you have to start at the battle's beginning: Fort Abraham Lincoln.

Almost every American has heard of General George Armstrong Custer and his famous defeat. What is it about the event that continues to draw so many people to an isolated corner of Montana to walk in the shadows of the 7th Cavalry? It is not just our own citizens who are fascinated with the Last Stand; history buffs from all over the world make the pilgrimage. Obviously something is special about the causes, the place, the people involved, and the aftermath of the battle that has held our collective attention for almost 150 years.

Perhaps it is the uniqueness of the situation that makes the Battle of the Little Bighorn stand out. Rarely before were so many soldiers sent to confront such a large gathering of Native Americans in one place. Never before had the American people been so totally shocked by the results of a battle few even knew was taking place. In July 1876, at the height of the centennial celebration of our nation's founding, news that the "Boy General" of the Civil War was lying dead on the Northern Plains was just too much to comprehend.

The mystery of what happened in the last hours of the battle certainly contributes to the ongoing fascination. None of the soldiers in Custer's battalion lived to tell the tale. The battalions assigned to Major Reno and Captain Benteen were not in a position to see the final moments of the action. The conflicting testimonies of these soldiers in the days, months, and years that followed did little to clear the fog of war. Likewise, the Lakota and Cheyenne warriors engaged with Custer's troops often gave differing accounts of what happened. Oral histories from the native warriors, passed down through their descendants, survive. After so many years, though, it is difficult to separate fact from myth. Modern archeology and forensic science have opened new venues of exploration and study. Ballistics testing, for example, can now allow researchers to follow the movements of a specific weapon across the battlefield.[1] However, for every old question answered, new questions arise. In all likelihood, fifty years from now we'll have even more unanswered questions than we do today.

---

[1]Douglas Scott, et al., *Archaeological Perspectives on the Battle of the Little Bighorn* (Norman: University of Oklahoma Press, 1989).

Since the first bodies of the cavalry troops were found strewn about Last Stand Hill, Deep Ravine, Battle Ridge, and a host of other now famous landmarks on the battlefield, people have been asking how and why. To meet the demand for answers, authors have been churning out books regularly since 1876. Historian Robert Utley wrote, "An oft-repeated cliché in military history circles is, 'More words have been written about the Battle of the Little Bighorn than any battle except Gettysburg.'"[2] Utley himself was not sure of the validity of the statement, but it does demonstrate how enormous the body of literature is. These works generally fall into one of two categories: a discussion about tactics or an analysis of Custer's character. It should be noted, however, that recent books have expanded the scope of discussion by bringing to light the contributions of other battlefield participants. One such book I particularly enjoyed was *Deliverance from the Little Bighorn: Doctor Henry Porter and Custer's Seventh Cavalry*, by Joan Nabseth Stevenson.

What still receives little attention, however, is the path Custer took from Fort Abraham Lincoln (in 1876, the home of the 7th Cavalry) to his final reckoning on the battlefield. Six hundred cavalrymen did not suddenly arrive on the scene without a great deal of effort. Yet of the hundreds of books written, I know of only two that ever addressed the 7th Cavalry's route in any detail. Both books were produced in limited numbers and both are now, sadly, out of print.

From the 1930s into the 1950s, North Dakota native Frank Anders surveyed Custer's route. Anders was born at Fort Abraham Lincoln while Custer commanded its garrison. His father was an infantryman stationed at the fort. Lieutenant Edward Godfrey, who survived the Battle of the Little Bighorn on Reno Hill, was Anders's godfather. Frank was a year old when he watched Custer march away.

Anders's own military career began in 1894 when he enlisted in the North Dakota National Guard. Five years later he was awarded the Medal of Honor for his service in the Philippines. When he re-

turned home, Anders enrolled in college and earned an engineering degree. He eventually became the City Engineer of Fargo. Soon after the onset of US involvement in World War I, Frank Anders was commissioned as a Captain in the Corps of Engineers. In 1921, he served as an honorary pallbearer at the interment of the Unknown Soldier in Arlington National Cemetery.

Given Anders's beginnings at Fort Abraham Lincoln and his ties to the soldiers stationed there, it's likely his interest in Custer and the 7th Cavalry began at an early age. During his own service in the military, he was tasked with writing various camp histories. It was probably inevitable that he would sooner or later take up Custer's trail.

Frank Anders was many things in life. Unfortunately, he was not an author in the conventional sense. He wrote many articles for engineering and historical journals but never quite got around to compiling his thirty years of research into a single book. Anders died in 1966. Luckily for us, his notes regarding Custer's most famous march survived.

Two years before Anders's death, an article appeared in the journal *North Dakota History* that summarized the route Custer took as he headed west to the Little Bighorn.[3] The authors, Gordon and Beth Bell, cited the "unpublished notes" of Major Frank Anders as one of their key sources. No maps were included, and the scope of the article ended at the Montana state line.

In 1983, John Carroll edited Mr. Anders's work and published *The Custer Trail: A Narrative of the Line of March of Troops Serving in the Department of Dakota in the Campaign Against Hostile Sioux, 1876*. Only 350 copies were printed, and each copy was numbered and signed. They are extremely difficult to find today.

Carroll was a noted historian and author of many Custer-related books, including *The Two Battles of the Little Bighorn* (1974), *General Custer and the Battle of the Little Bighorn* (1985), and *They Rode with Custer* (1987). He was also credited as the historical con-

---

[2]Robert M. Utley, Foreword to *Custer, the Seventh Cavalry, and the Little Big Horn: A Bibliography,* ed. Michael O'Keefe (Glendale: The Arthur H. Clark Company, 2012).

[3]Gordon Bell and Beth L. Gordon, "General Custer in North Dakota," *North Dakota History: Journal of the Northern Plains* 31, No. 2 (1964).

sultant for the 1991 television mini-series *Son of the Morning Star*. He passed away in 1990 shortly before the mini-series first aired. Because of his service in the US Air Force and his extensive research surrounding the Battle of the Little Bighorn, John Carroll was buried in the Custer National Cemetery at the battlefield. Each year, the Little Big Horn Associates, Inc., presents the John Carroll Award to the best new book about Custer or the Little Bighorn battle.

In 1997, travel agent and amateur historian Laudie Chorne updated the work of Anders and Carroll by publishing *Following the Custer Trail of 1876*. This title seems to have been published by multiple companies. I own the Third Edition, by Trails West, Bismarck, North Dakota, 1997.

Chorne was born in South Heart, North Dakota, in 1929 and spent most of his life in North Dakota, Montana, and Idaho. He worked a few years with Frontier Airlines before starting his own travel agency in Dickinson, North Dakota. After selling the agency, Chorne began writing articles for various history-themed journals. *Following the Custer Trail of 1876* was his only book. While currently out of print, copies of various editions are readily available on the used-book market. Laudie Chorne died in 2013.

In science it is often said we see farther by standing on the shoulders of giants. By education and by vocation I am a biologist, not a historian. My work here sets squarely on the foundations laid earlier by Anders, Carroll, and Chorne. This book, however, takes advantage of several modern technologies that were unavailable to the previous authors. First and foremost is the development of the Global Positioning System (GPS). I have provided the GPS coordinates of Custer's campsites and a few significant landmarks found along the route. Also given are the GPS coordinates where each photograph was taken. Anyone with a computer, a GPS receiver, or an appropriate smartphone application can quickly pinpoint these locations. The earlier authors referred to Sections, Townships, and Ranges. Very few people today, with the possible exception of land surveyors and tax assessors, know how to use that information.

A few words about GPS coordinates may be appropriate at this point. Historically, latitude and longitude were expressed in Degrees, Minutes, and Seconds (D/M/S). The coordinates for latitude are always given before longitude. As we moved into a digital world, the format Degrees, Digital Minutes (D/DM) became more common. Today, with the transition to digital almost complete, the format of Digital Degrees (DD) is gaining popularity. For example, the location of the Custer House at Fort Abraham Lincoln can be expressed in D/M/S as 46°45'32.58"N, 100°50'49.42"W. In the D/DM format, the same location would be shown as 46°45.543'N, 100°50.824'W. Finally, the coordinates for the Custer House given in the DD format would be 46.759177, -100.847070. Note the abbreviations "N" and the "W" for the northern and western hemispheres are not used in the DD format. Instead, a minus sign (-) indicates either the southern or western hemispheres. For this guide, I have chosen to use the DD format because it is the easiest to use when inputting a location into a mobile device.

The second recent technology I have embraced is digital maps. The US Geological Survey now makes all their new 7.5-degree topographical maps available for download free from the website: https://viewer.nationalmap.gov/launch/. Note that web addresses do change over time. With a little practice, anyone can print an entire map or select just the areas they need. The names of the topographic maps used for this book are listed, in sequence from east to west, in the Appendix.

The last modern technology I have the advantage of using is digital printing. Whereas Chorne's book used grainy black-and-white copies of maps and old photographs, I have been able to include full color maps and photographs of each site. All of the photographs were taken by me in June and July 2018, or in September 2019. Digital printing technology also allows the placement of color illustrations throughout the book rather than on separate plates.

The maps used in this book, with the exception of the fold-out overview map, are all public domain maps obtained from the US

Geological Survey. Unlike most older topographic maps, however, the spacing of the grid lines on these newer maps is one thousand meters. The resulting squares represent one square kilometer of land. Anders's maps often did not include grid lines, and when he did draw them the spacing varied. The maps used by Chorne had grid-squares, which represented one section of land and were usually annotated with the section numbers. In US land surveys, one section of land is equal to one square mile. These are important differences to remember when comparing older and newer maps. All of the maps included in this book use a contour interval of ten feet. Any annotations I have made on the maps and photographs are shown in bold or red text.

The primary purpose of this book is to enable the reader to find each site Custer camped at along the way to the Little Bighorn. It is not my intention to dwell on the specifics of Custer's personality, the order of march, or the tactics of the battle; other writers have done that *ad infinitum*. I would like to set the stage, however, for readers who may not be as well versed in all things Custer.

George Armstrong Custer was a West Point graduate and a decorated cavalry officer of the American Civil War. He personally led numerous charges against enemy forces and developed a reputation for bravery, flamboyance, and luck. During that war, he received brevet promotions first to brigadier general and then to major general. At the time, brevet promotions were occasionally given to soldiers for gallantry or exceptional service. A brevet rank was honorary; it granted no additional authority or pay. At the end of the Civil War, Custer's official rank in the Regular Army was captain. Following a short tour of duty in Texas, he took an extended leave of absence while awaiting new orders in the downsized Regular Army.

On July 28, 1866, Custer received his orders. He was appointed lieutenant colonel and assigned to the newly created US 7th Cavalry. For the remainder of his life, he served as a cavalry officer on the Great Plains. Of his many talents, self-promotion was among his best. He routinely wrote letters and articles and books highlighting his adventures. In the 1870s, Custer's exploits were well-known in Eastern US cities.

Following the Civil War, the struggle for land on the Northern Plains heated up. The Panic of 1873 caused an economic depression that spurred many people to abandon their homes and move west. The discovery of gold in the Black Hills of modern South Dakota in 1874 only exacerbated the situation. The US Government tried to renegotiate the Laramie Treaty of 1868, which had set aside the Black Hills for the Sioux. This was sacred ground to the Sioux and they were not in the mood to cede any more of their land. Fights between the Indians and the intruders were inevitable. The US Government came to believe the only way to bring peace to the region was to gather all the various native tribes onto reservations. Most tribes complied, but a large number of Sioux and their allies, the Northern Cheyenne, continued to resist. On December 3, 1875, Secretary of the Interior Zachariah Chandler instructed his agents of the Bureau of Indian Affairs to inform Sitting Bull and other tribal chiefs that all remaining Indians had to report to their respective reservations by January 31, 1876, or the matter would be turned over to the War Department. The deadline came and went. On February 1, 1876, Chandler sent a letter to Secretary of War William Belknap that stated, in part,

> The time given him in which to return to an agency having expired, and the advice received at the Indian Office being to the effect that Sitting Bull still refuses to comply with the direction of the Commissioner, the said Indians are hereby turned over to the War Department for such action on the part of the Army as you may deem proper under the circumstances. I inclose copy of the communication from the Commissioner of Indian Affairs, dated the 31 ultimo, recommending that hostilities be commenced.[4]

Thus, the stage was set for the Great Sioux War of 1876.

---

[4]Secretary of the Interior to the Secretary of War, February 1, 1876, National Archives.

Because so many Indians had failed to comply with the instructions of the Indian agents, the army devised a plan that, if successful, would round up all the Indians with one large campaign and force them back onto their reservations. Three large columns of troops would march onto the Northern Plains where it was believed the Indians were camped. One column, under the command of Brigadier General George Crook, was to head north from Fort Fetterman, Wyoming. A second column, under the command of Colonel John Gibbon, was directed to move eastward from Fort Ellis, Montana. The third column, under the command of Brigadier General Alfred Terry, was ordered to march west from Fort Abraham Lincoln, North Dakota.

There was never any intention that these forces would meet up and conduct an epic battle with the Indians. There were just too many unknowns. First, nobody could be certain how many Indians were out on the plains. Government agents routinely overestimated the number of Indians on the reservations for various reasons. This meant the number of Indians off the reservations was almost always underestimated. Second, the army could not know exactly where these Indians were at any given time. The lifestyle of the tribes meant they were frequently on the move. The army expected to find Sitting Bull's camp on one of the tributaries that flowed north towards the Yellowstone River, but exactly which tributary was the big question. The hope was that one of the columns would eventually find the Indians and drive them into one of the other columns and force a surrender.

The bulk of General Terry's column consisted of twelve companies (about six hundred men) of the 7th Cavalry, commanded by Custer. The remainder of the column consisted of infantry, engineers, civilian teamsters, and Arikara scouts (the Arikara tribesmen were enemies of the Lakota Sioux and were more than willing to help the army find them). In all, approximately 1,200 men, 1,800 animals, and 150 wagons made up the Dakota Column.

It would be a mistake to assume the Dakota Column was venturing west into uncharted territory. In fact, five other sizable military expeditions preceded Terry's into the region. While the Dakota Column did not follow any of the earlier routes completely, it did use segments of all of them at one time or another. The scars left on the prairie by so many troops and animals were not soon erased. Custer had only to follow the signs.

In 1864, General Alfred Sully led approximately 2,200 troops west from Fort Rice, Dakota Territory, to the Little Missouri badlands and then northward before circling back to Fort Rice. His trail west was a bit south of Custer's 1876 route, but the paths did cross at several points. Sully's troops were the first large group of soldiers to enter the badlands. They followed a stream that would later be named Sully Creek. When Sully reached the Little Missouri River, he turned south and marched about two miles before establishing camp at the mouth of Davis Creek. The Dakota Column camped in the same spot twelve years later. As Sully's troops climbed out of the badlands on the west side, they had several skirmishes with Sioux warriors. The Battle of the Badlands took place around Flat Top Butte (called Square Butte on modern maps), less than three miles south of Custer's 1876 "Snow Camp." The main consequence of the Battle of the Badlands was that it pushed the bulk of the Sioux farther west into the Powder River basin.

Even as the Civil War raged on, plans for a railroad to link the Great Lakes to the Puget Sound were being considered. As survey crews sought out the best route through the Dakota and Montana Territories, they were repeatedly attacked by Indians. In 1871, Major Joseph Whistler escorted the Northern Pacific Railroad surveyors with seven infantry companies, approximately 450 men. It is believed they approached the Little Missouri River via Davis Creek.[5]

The following year, Colonel David Stanley escorted the surveyors with six hundred infantrymen. Hoping to avoid the badlands

---

[5] US Forest Service, History and Culture of the Dakota Prairie Grasslands.

altogether, they traveled about twenty-five miles south of Whistler's trail. They found this route to be even worse. Passing into Montana, they came to Beaver Creek and followed it south to near its origin. Turning west again, they made their way to O'Fallon Creek and followed it downstream to the Yellowstone River. A few years later, the Dakota Column would take a similar route from Beaver Creek to O'Fallon Creek but continue west to the Powder River.

In 1873, Colonel Stanley took a much larger force to escort the surveyors. This time they followed Whistler's 1871 route. As Stanley headed out from the newly constructed Fort Abraham Lincoln, he commanded over two thousand men. In addition to the infantry, he was joined by ten companies of the 7th Cavalry led by Lieutenant Colonel Custer. The expedition again approached the Little Missouri River by following Davis Creek. After crossing the Little Missouri, they ascended out of the badlands, passed Flat Top and Sentinel Buttes, and headed for the Yellowstone River along the divide that separates Glendive Creek from Cedar Creek. Six miles south (upriver) from present day Glendive, Montana, Stanley established a supply depot, which eventually came to be known as Stanley's Stockade. Three years later, Terry and Custer would use this same depot as a supply base for their Dakota Column.

In 1874, Custer finally led an expedition of his own. With ten companies of his 7th Cavalry, he brought along engineers, scientists, miners, correspondents, and one photographer. Their goal was to explore the Black Hills in today's South Dakota. It was on this expedition that the presence of gold was confirmed. As they returned to Fort Abraham Lincoln, they moved north on the west side of the Little Missouri River, turned east through the badlands, and traveled home along Stanley's 1873 route. Custer's training for his ultimate march was now complete.

On the chilly, foggy morning of May 17, 1876, Terry's column departed Fort Abraham Lincoln. With Custer and his cavalry in the lead, the regimental band played the tune "Garryowen" as farewells were made. In a surreal omen of things to come, a rare atmospheric phenomenon occurred. As the troops marched off to the west with the music of "The Girl I Left Behind Me" wafting through the valley, the low cloud cover combined with the rays of the morning sun to produce a ghostly reflection of the troops in the sky above the fort.

Between Fort Lincoln and the Little Bighorn, Custer established twenty-seven campsites as he traveled west. Today, most of the sites are on private land. All but three of the locations, however, are easily accessible and visible from public roadways. With the accuracy of GPS, one could possibly imagine the camps as distinct points. This would not be correct. In reality, each campsite was irregularly shaped and many acres in size. Not only were 600 to 1,200 men pitching tents, cooking, bathing, and doing all the things soldiers do in the field, 1,800 animals were also grazing nearby. When viewing a campsite, it is important to visualize the area as a whole rather than focusing on a single point.

Again, the goal of this book is to simply help the reader *find* the campsites. To anyone traveling along Custer's path from Fort Abraham Lincoln to the Little Bighorn Battlefield, I would highly recommend carrying a copy of *Following the Custer Trail of 1876*, by Laudie Chorne. Although his maps and photographs are dated by today's standards, the background information he provided will make the trip much more meaningful.

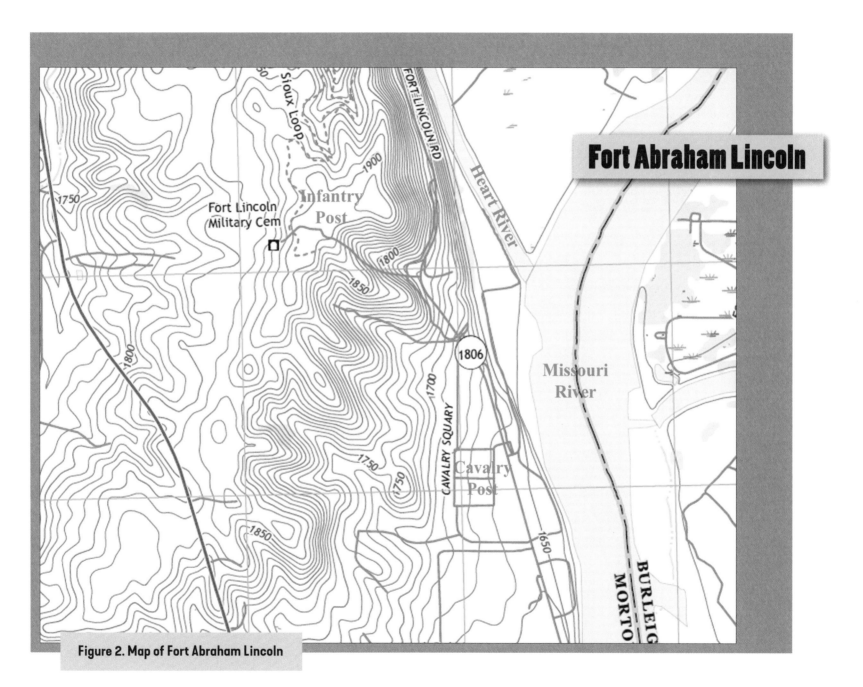

Figure 2. Map of Fort Abraham Lincoln

Fort Abraham Lincoln

General Location: 5.0 miles south of Mandan, North Dakota

Ownership Status: public (North Dakota State Park)

GPS Coordinates:

> Entrance Gate: 46.756123, -100.841838
>
> Cavalry Post: 46.759140, -100.845542
>
> Infantry Post: 46.770286, -100.853018

Directions:

1. From Bismarck, drive west on I-94 to Exit 153

2. Turn south (left) onto Mandan Avenue and go 0.8 miles

3. Turn west (right) onto Main Street and go 0.5 miles

4. Turn south (left) onto 6th Avenue SE (ND Hwy 1806) and go 7.0 miles

5. Turn north (left) onto Fort Lincoln Road and go 0.6 miles to the Entrance Gate

Fort Abraham Lincoln began as an infantry post named Fort McKeen in the spring of 1872. It was originally designed to garrison three companies of infantry. On November 19, 1872, the fort was renamed Fort Abraham Lincoln. The following year, the fort was expanded, and an additional six companies of cavalry were authorized to be garrisoned there. Although the fort had a combined force of nine companies with a single post commander, the infantry and the cavalry quarters remained separate. The infantry occupied the bluff above the confluence of the Heart and Missouri Rivers, and the cavalry was located in the valley next to the Missouri. The two sub-posts were separated by about one mile. Over seventy-five permanent buildings were eventually constructed.

The six companies of cavalry at Fort Abraham Lincoln represented half of the US Army's 7th Cavalry Regiment. The balance of the regiment's companies was stationed at other outposts throughout the country. The 7th Cavalry's deputy commander, Lieutenant Colonel George Armstrong Custer, had the additional duty of serving as the expanded fort's first post commander.

As preparations were being made for the departure of the Dakota Column from Fort Lincoln in 1876, additional troops and supplies were transferred to the post. All twelve companies of the 7th Cavalry were brought together for the first time since 1868. They were joined by two companies of the 17th Infantry (companies C and G), one company of the 6th Infantry (Company B), a detached battery of three Gatling gun crews from the 20th Infantry, and an assortment of military and civilian support personnel.[6] All of the new temporary arrivals were housed in tents on the fort. Additionally, the six companies of cavalry already garrisoned at the fort were removed from their barracks and put into tents south of the post.[7]

---

[6]From newspaperman Mark Kellogg's first article relating his travels with the 7th Cavalry, *Bismarck* [ND] *Tribune*, May 17, 1876.

[7]Elizabeth B. Custer, *"Boots and Saddles" or Life in Dakota with General Custer* (London: American Cowboy Books, 2015), Kindle.

Commanding the Dakota Column was Brigadier General Alfred Terry. He was the commander of the Department of Dakota and was based at Fort Snelling, Minnesota. He arrived at Fort Abraham Lincoln shortly before the column's departure. The actual commander of the 7th Cavalry was Colonel Samuel Sturgis, but he was on detached duty in St. Louis at the time. This put Custer in the role of acting commander of the 7th Cavalry during the campaign.

On the morning of May 17, 1876, most of the Dakota Column had been previously staged on the bluff near the infantry post. The cavalry, however, was still positioned in the valley below. With Custer in the lead, the 7th Cavalry conducted a formal parade through their post before ascending the bluff to join the rest of the column. Accompanying Custer were his wife, Libbie, and his sister Maggie, who was married to Lieutenant James Calhoun of the 7th Cavalry. As they reached the top of the bluff, they gazed back toward the cavalry post below. It was from this point that the reflection of the approaching troops was seen in the low clouds above. "As the sun broke through the mist," Libbie Custer later wrote,

> a mirage appeared, which took up about half of the line of cavalry, and thenceforth for a little distance it marched, equally plain to the sight on the land and in the sky. The future of the heroic band, whose days were even then numbered, seemed to be revealed, and already there seemed a premonition in the supernatural translation as their forms were reflected in the opaque mist of the early dawn.[8]

---

[8]Ibid.

Figure 3. A reconstruction of the
Custer House at Fort Abraham Lincoln

Figure 4. A reconstructed Cavalry Barracks at Fort Abraham Lincoln

Figure 5. One of three reconstructed blockhouses on the Infantry Post at Fort Abraham Lincoln

Figure 6. The Cavalry Post, as seen from the Infantry Post at Fort Abraham Lincoln. It was from this point that Libbie Custer and others reported seeing the reflection of the approaching cavalry troops in the clouds above the valley as the Dakota Column began their march.

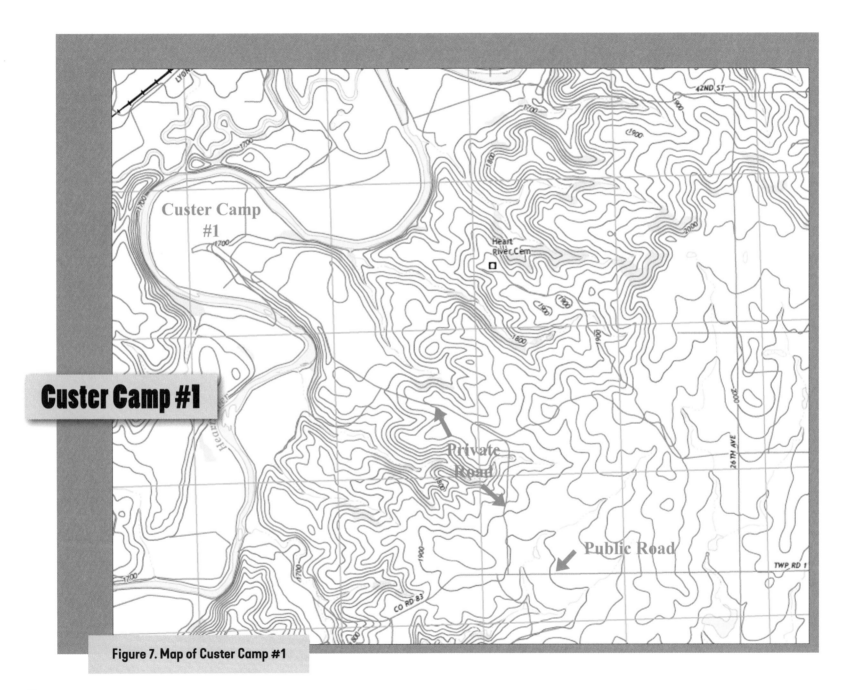

Custer Camp #1

Figure 7. Map of Custer Camp #1

Custer Camp #1

May 17, 1876

General Location: 8.2 miles west of Mandan, North Dakota

Ownership Status:
private property; access requires prior permission from landowner

GPS Coordinates: 46.797675, -101.055406

Directions:

1. From the entrance gate at Fort Abraham Lincoln State Park, go south on Fort Lincoln Road 0.6 miles to North Dakota Highway 1806.

2. Turn northwest (right) onto ND 1806 and go 2.4 miles to County Road 138.

3. Turn west (left) onto CR 138 and go 3.8 miles to 23rd Avenue.

4. Turn north (right) onto 23rd Avenue and go 1.0 miles to Township Road 1.

5. Turn west (left) onto TWP RD 1 and go 4.0 miles to a private road.

6. If you have permission to enter the private property, turn north (right) onto the private road and go 2.0 miles until the road ends at a private home. This is the site of Custer's first campsite.

The site of Custer's first camp after his departure from Fort Abraham Lincoln is situated on private land and cannot be seen from a public roadway. In 1997, author Chorne described a gate that had to be crossed, followed by a one-mile hike. He said nothing about "No Trespassing" signs at the time. Currently the land is posted. It is owned by Mr. Wes Pulkrabek of Mandan, North Dakota. He gave me a tour of the site in September 2019 and expressed his willingness to allow others to view it. The land is a working farm, however, so he insists that visitors make arrangements with him first before coming onto the property. For privacy reasons, I'm not supplying his address or phone number here. However, a determined visitor can easily find the information online.

As the Dakota Column's various elements took their assigned positions in the line of march, Custer led the way. They covered just over thirteen miles on the first day, most of it over easy terrain. On some modern maps a portion of their route crossed an area now labeled as "Custer Flats." Custer knew better than to pay the soldiers right before leaving on a long campaign. With all the saloons and bordellos in nearby Bismarck, the chances were too great that some of his troops would not be fit for duty at the hour of departure. The troops would receive their pay when they arrived at the Heart River, a safe distance from temptation. Arrangements had been made for Custer's wife, Libbie, and his sister, Maggie Calhoun, to accompany the column to the first night's camp on the Heart River and then return to Fort Abraham Lincoln the next day with the paymaster's wagon.

The site of the first day's camp was within a wide curve of the Heart River. It was chosen because of its proximity to a well-known ford. On satellite images, the ford is still visible southeast of the campsite. If you have permission to visit the site, you can also see that the west bank of the Heart River is still cut down at the ford to permit easy crossing.

Figure 8. Custer Camp #1 is located at the end of this private road. As noted in the text, the site may be visited only if prior permission to enter the property is obtained from the landowner. (photo location: GPS 46.776756, -101.027989, facing north)

Custer Camp #1

Heart River

Figure 9. Custer Camp #1 was located within a bend of the Heart River. The site is now a private farm. (photo location: GPS 46.796916, -101.047482, facing northwest)

Heart River Ford

Figure 10. Departing from their first campsite on the morning of May 18, 1876, the Dakota Column crossed the Heart River at a ford that is still in use today. Note the cut on the opposite embankment. (photo location: GPS 46.793596, -101.049446, facing south)

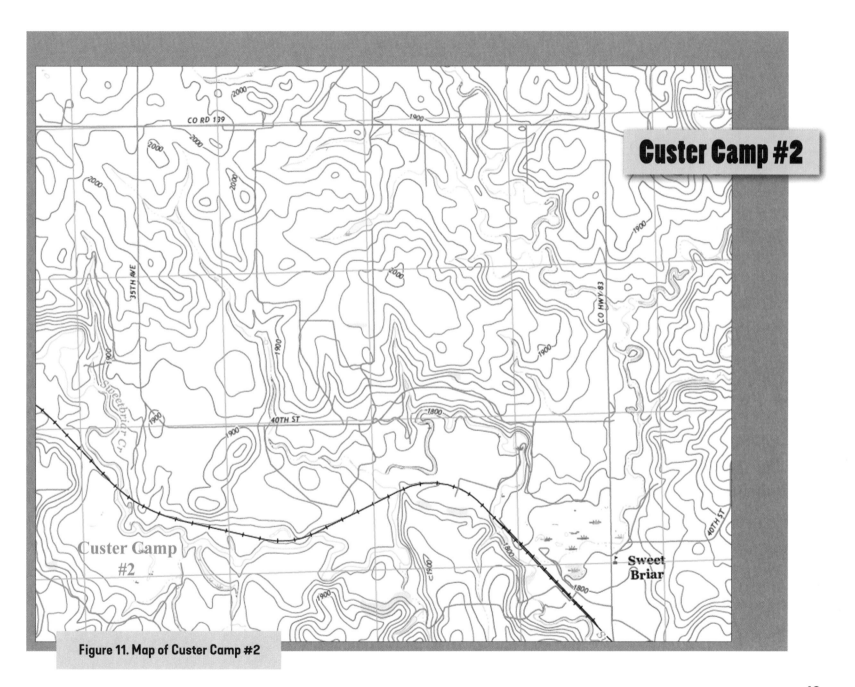

Custer Camp #2

Custer Camp
#2

Sweet
Briar

Figure 11. Map of Custer Camp #2

Custer Camp #2

May 18, 1876

General Location: 4.0 miles east of Judson, North Dakota

Ownership Status: private property but visible from public road

GPS Coordinates: 46.825102, -101.198235

Directions:

1. From I-94 West, take Exit 140 to County Road 83.

2. Turn south (left) onto County Road 83 and go 0.8 miles.

3. Turn west (right) onto County Road 139 (Old Hwy 10) and go 2.0 miles.

4. Turn south (left) onto 35th Avenue and go 0.5 miles to the top of a hill. This is the best vantage point to see Custer's second campsite. From this hilltop, the site is straight south another 1.3 miles. It is just beyond the modern railroad tracks and Sweetbriar Creek.

5. If you want to get closer, continue south on 35th Avenue for another 0.5 miles until the road takes a sharp turn to the east. Look south and you'll see an old two-story farmhouse. Custer's second camp was located slightly north and west of that house.

Reveille sounded just after 2:30 a.m. at the Heart River camp. Although the river ford was solid, the banks on either side were steep and soft. It was difficult enough for the horses and the foot soldiers, but alterations had to be made before the wagons could cross. Cuts in the embankments were dug, and logs were laid astride the path so the wagons' wheels would not sink into the sandy mud. It was mid-morning before the entire column made it to the opposite side of the river.

Custer waited until everything was across the water before he said his final goodbyes to Libbie. He watched until she and Maggie, along with the paymaster and their escorts, were over the hills to the east and out of sight. It would be his last gaze upon his wife. He then moved to the head of the column and the march resumed.

As the crow flies, the Dakota Column only covered about seven miles on their second day of travel. The actual distance was a little longer due to their maneuvering around various streams and terrain features. The first men reached camp shortly after 2:00 p.m., but the last wagons didn't roll into camp until just past 6:00 p.m. according to General Terry's journal.

Custer Camp #2

Figure 12. Custer Camp #2 is best viewed from a hilltop along 35th Avenue south of County Road 139. (photo location: GPS 46.843139, -101.197708, facing south)

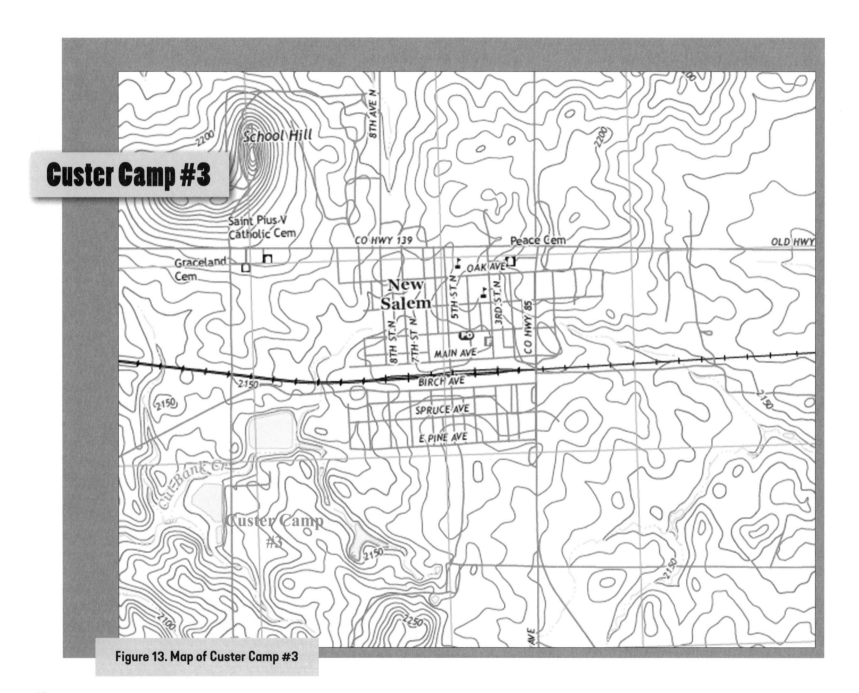

Figure 13. Map of Custer Camp #3

Custer Camp #3

May 19, 1876

General Location: Southwest corner of New Salem, North Dakota

Ownership Status: private property but visible from public road

GPS Coordinates: 46.834316, -101.426640

Directions:

1. From I-94 West, take Exit 127 to 8th Street (ND Hwy 31).

2. Turn south (left) onto 8th Street and go 1.0 miles to Ash Avenue (CR 139).

3. Turn east (left) onto Ash Avenue and go 0.2 miles to 5th Avenue.

4. Turn south (right) onto 5th Avenue and go 0.4 miles to Birch Avenue.

5. Turn west (right) onto Birch Avenue and go 0.7 miles to 48th Avenue.

6. Turn south (left) onto 48th Avenue and go 0.4 miles. Custer's third campsite was on the east (left) side of the road next to the small stream.

Custer's third camp was located just southwest of New Salem along a small creek identified on modern maps as Cut Bank Creek. It was unnamed and essentially dry when the Dakota Column camped here. With very little water, many of the men went without dinner or coffee after they arrived in camp. Likewise, few bothered to cook breakfast the next morning.

A mile north of this camp was Crow's Nest Butte, a familiar landmark of the time. Today, the feature is known as School Hill. In 1974, a new adornment was added: "Salem Sue" is a fiberglass Holstein cow which stands thirty-eight feet tall and reportedly cost $40,000 when she was constructed. Salem Sue can be seen for miles around.

Figure 14. Custer Camp #3 as seen from 48th Avenue, southwest of New Salem, ND. (photo location: GPS 46.831499, -101.427605, facing north)

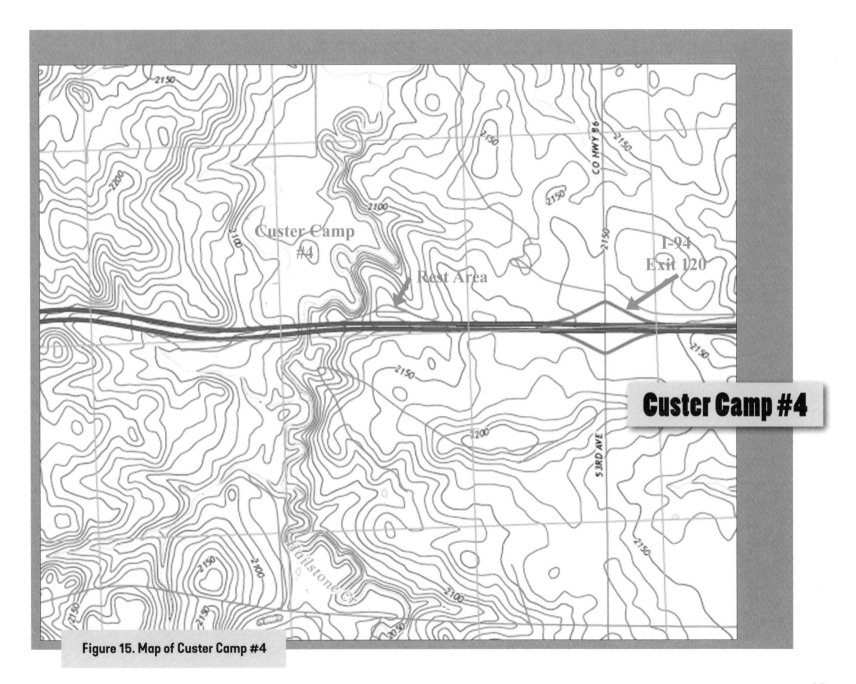

Figure 15. Map of Custer Camp #4

Custer Camp #4

May 20, 1876

General Location: 8.6 miles west of New Salem, North Dakota

Ownership Status:
private property but visible from public highway rest area

GPS Coordinates: 46.865280, -101.595812

Directions:
Follow I-94 west to the Rest Area located 0.7 miles west of Exit 120.

This is one of the easier camps to see. Stop at the highway rest area. The campsite was located on Hailstone Creek, which is visible down the slope from the main building. The deck on the north side of the building provides an excellent view.

As the Dakota Column pressed on, rain hampered their movement throughout the day. Only nine and a half miles were covered between the third and fourth camps. Hailstone Creek is a modern name. General Terry, in his journal, referred to it only as "another branch of the Big Muddy." While camp was being established along the creek, lightning struck. One of the Gatling gun teams stampeded. Only minor damage was done, but the horses traveled a mile before they were caught.

Custer Camp #4

Figure 16. Custer Camp #4 is best viewed from the deck of the I-94 West rest area, west of Exit 120. (photo location: GPS 46.862744, -101.591499, looking northwest)

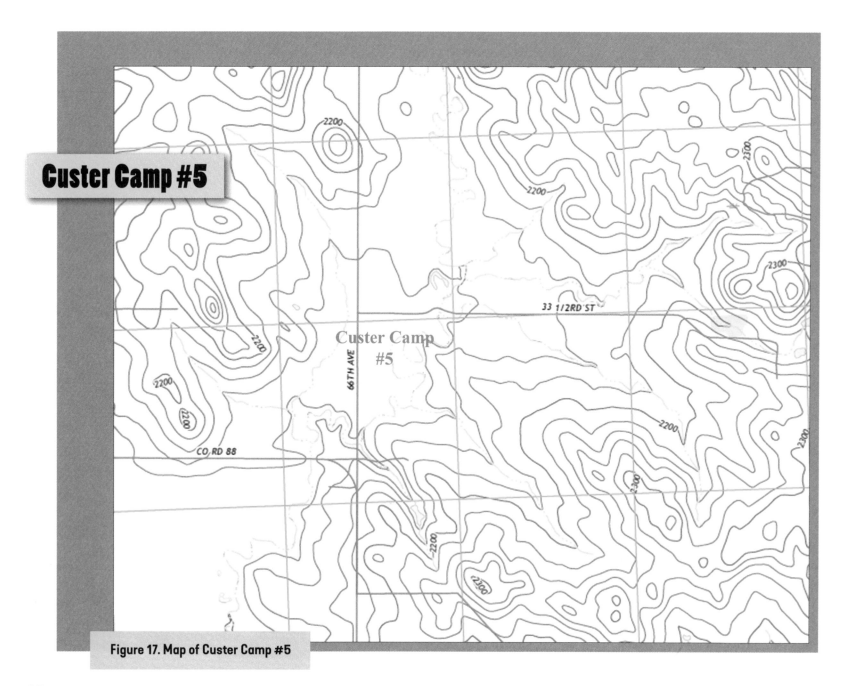

Custer Camp #5

Custer Camp
#5

Figure 17. Map of Custer Camp #5

Custer Camp #5

May 21, 1876

General Location: 7.5 miles north of Glen Ullin, North Dakota

Ownership Status: private property but visible from public road

GPS Coordinates: 46.927700, -101.839506

Directions:

1. From I-94 West, take Exit 108 to County Road 88.

2. Turn north (right) onto CR 88 and go 4.2 miles.

3. At this point, CR 88 makes a sharp turn to the west (left) and 66th Avenue continues straight northward. Camp #5 was located about a quarter mile northeast of this intersection along a tributary to Haymarsh Creek.

Although the day started cold and misty, as had most mornings since leaving Fort Abraham Lincoln, by noon the sun was shining. Morale seemed to instantly improve. Consequently, the Dakota Column was able to march almost fourteen miles before stopping at their fifth camp of the campaign.

As the troops marched northwest, in the south they could see the distinctive Twin Buttes. The Arikara scouts that were accompanying the column, however, knew the buttes by a more colorful name: Young Maiden's Breasts.[9] Mark Kellogg, the newspaper reporter from Bismarck who had joined the expedition, in his diary entry for May 21 wrote, "General Country rolling but with many high buttes with peculiar names given by the Indians viz. Rattlesnake Den, Wolfs Den, Cherry Ridge, Maidens Breasts." Kellogg mentions the landmark again, without further elaboration, in his third dispatch to the *Bismarck Tribune*, published on June 14, 1876.

[9]Orin G. Libby, *The Arikara Narrative of the Campaign Against the Hostile Dakotas*, June 1876 (Bismarck: North Dakota State Historical Society, 1920), 60.

Figure 18. Twin Buttes, known to the Arikara as the Young Maiden's Breasts. (photo location: GPS 46.843168, -101.717734, facing northeast)

Custer Camp #5

Figure 19. Custer Camp #5, viewed from the intersection of County Road 88 and 66th Avenue. (photo location: GPS 46.920314, -101.844635, facing north)

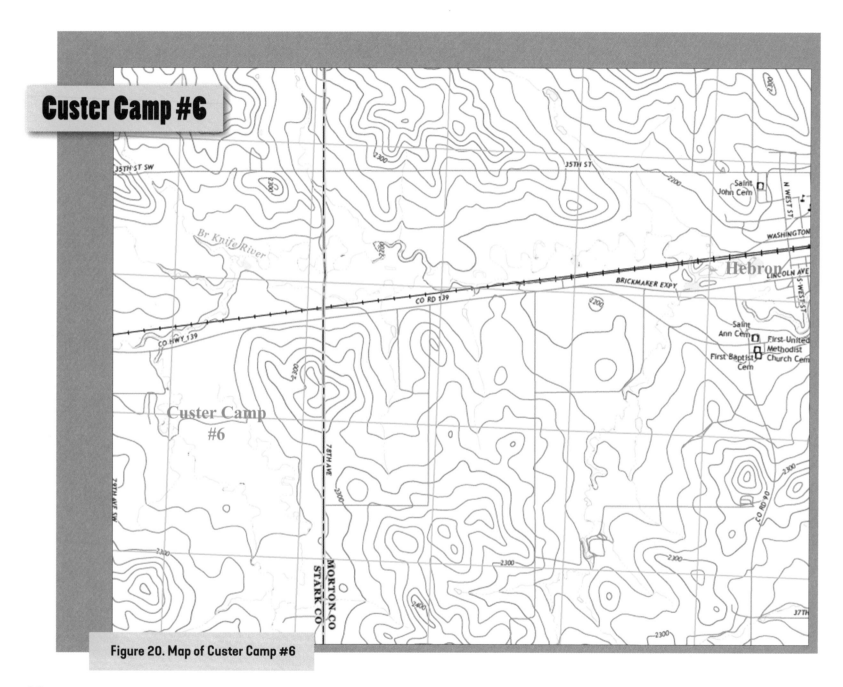

Custer Camp #6

Figure 20. Map of Custer Camp #6

Custer Camp #6

May 22, 1876

General Location: 2.9 miles west of Hebron, North Dakota

Ownership Status: private property but visible from public road

GPS Coordinates: 46.885011, -102.103243

Directions:

1. From I-94 West, take Exit 97 to County Road 90.

2. Turn north (right) onto CR 90 and go 2.2 miles to CR 139.

3. Turn west (left) onto CR 139 and go 2.6 miles.

4. At this point, Custer's camp was about 0.5 miles south (left), along the Branch Knife Creek.

As the Dakota Column approached this location, General Terry was concerned about the scarcity of wood and water ahead. Custer, of course, wanted to continue on. There was little water in the stream at the time, but steep banks on either side meant they would have to be dug down to a lesser grade before wagons could cross. During the crossing, one wagon overturned. The wagon was damaged, the cargo was spilled, and the driver was seriously injured. Because of the resulting delay, it was decided to halt where they were and establish camp early at 1:00 p.m.

Custer Camp #6

Figure 21. Custer Camp #6, as seen from County Road 139. (photo location: GPS 46.894572, -102.108221, facing south)

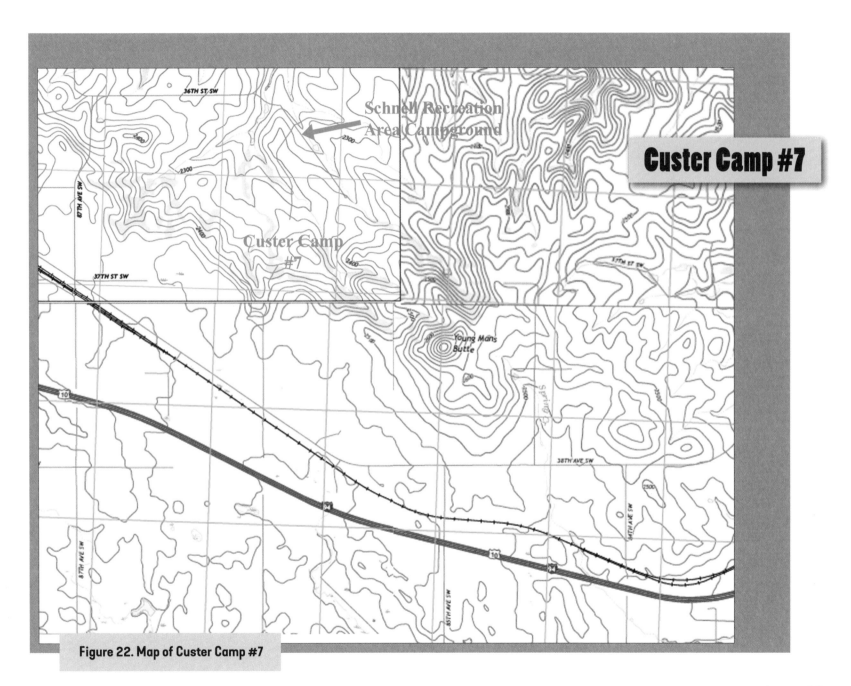

Custer Camp #7

Figure 22. Map of Custer Camp #7

Custer Camp #7

May 23, 1876

General Location: 2.5 miles east of Richardton, North Dakota

Ownership Status:
mix of private and public property but visible from public road

GPS Coordinates: 46.878000, -102.260871

Directions:

1. From I-94 West, take Exit 84 at Richardton to North Dakota Highway 8.

2. Turn north (right) onto ND 8 and go 0.7 miles.

3. Turn east (right) onto Old Highway 10 and go 1.1 miles to 87th Avenue SW (follow signs to Schnell Recreation Area).

4. Turn north (left) onto 87th Ave SW and go 1.1 miles to 36th Street SW.

5. Turn east (right) onto 36th St SW and go 1.0 miles to the Schnell Recreation Area. Custer's camp was approximately 0.5 miles south of the recreation area's campground.

Having traveled only eight miles since the sixth campsite, the seventh camp was made on the tablelands west of Young Man's Butte. The easiest way to observe the site today is to visit the campground at Schnell Recreation Area. When in the campground, look straight south and notice Young Man's Butte. This is the highest terrain feature in sight. Custer's camp was on the downward flanks to the right of the peak. There are hiking trails within the recreation area that can get you closer to the site, but they are often overgrown. Remember, this is rattlesnake country.

Unlike the previous camp, this camp had abundant fresh water and wood. Custer camped here two years earlier on his return from the Black Hills and was familiar with the area. The site is situated among several springs and small tributaries to the Knife River. Terry again ordered an early halt to allow the troops and animals to rest and take advantage of the "great abundance of wood, fine spring water, good grass."[10]

There are at least two different legends regarding the name Young Man's Butte. In 2018, Dakota Goodhouse shared with historian Tom Isern the following story:

> [a] long time ago, the Hunkpapha encountered a hunting party of Crow and, regarding them as trespassers, attacked. The last remaining Crow, a young man, ascended the butte in flight, and there took his own life in order to avoid capture by the Hunkpapha. Ever since, in his remembrance, Lakhota people have called this place Paha Khoskalaka, Young Man's Butte.[11]

In 1938, the Federal Writers' Project of the Works Progress Administration (WPA) produced a series of books including *North Dakota: A Guide to the Northern Prairie State*. Within its pages can

---

[10]Alfred Howe Terry, *The Terry Diary: Battle of the Little Bighorn* (Bellevue, WA: Big Byte Books), Kindle Edition 2014.

[11]Tom Isern, Young Man's Butte (Plains Folk audio broadcast), Prairie Public Broadcasting, August 28, 2018.

be found another account of the landmark's naming. Note that the WPA writers called it "Young Men's Butte" rather than "Young Man's Butte":

> According to legend, when the Arikara Indians were still living on the Grand River, in what is now South Dakota, a group separated from the tribe and set out toward the northwest to seek a new home. Two young men in the party, however, grew lonesome for the sweethearts they had left behind, and when they reached this butte they decided to return to their old home. The remainder of the party continued on the journey, and was never heard from again.[12]

[12]Works Progress Administration, *North Dakota: A Guide to the Northern Prairie State* (Bismarck: State Historical Society of North Dakota, 2014), 294.

Young Man's Butte

Custer Camp #7

Figure 23. Custer's seventh campsite was located on the tablelands northwest of Young Man's Butte. (photo location: GPS 46.891287, -102.267694, facing southeast)

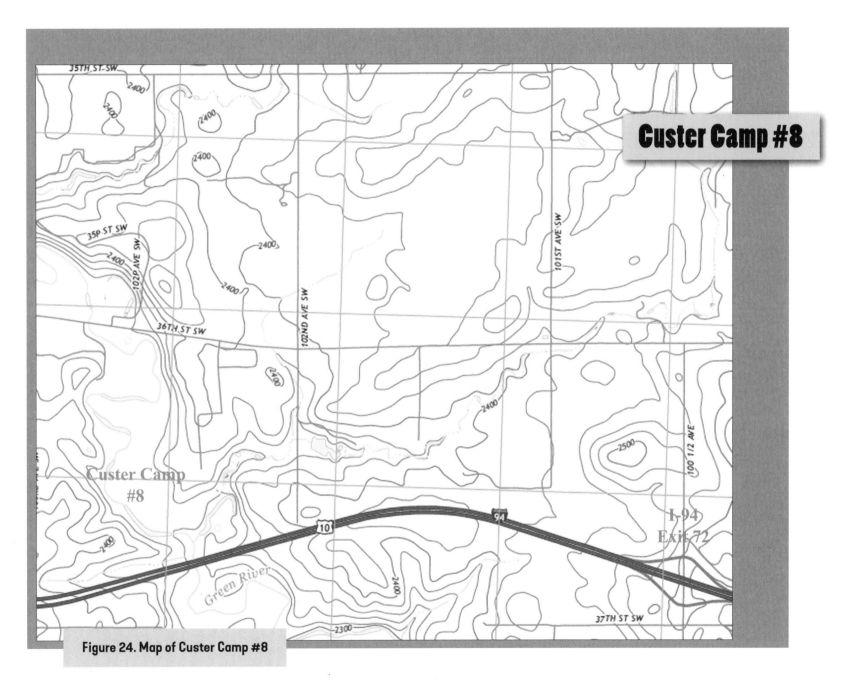

Custer Camp #8

Custer Camp
#8

Figure 24. Map of Custer Camp #8

Custer Camp #8

May 24, 1876

General Location: 2.7 miles northwest of Gladstone, North Dakota

Ownership Status: private property but visible from public road

GPS Coordinates: 46.883604, -102.613454

Directions:

1. From I-94 West, continue west from Exit 72 for another 1.9 miles.

2. At this point a bridge crosses the Green River. Custer's eighth camp was along the Green River just north (right) of the interstate.

This is another easy camp to find. It is visible on the north (right) side of I-94 West. According to Chorne, it was situated along the river the entire distance between I-94 and Old Highway 10 (36th Street SW) to the north. There used to be an interstate rest area on the east side of the river, but it was removed from service around 2009. Satellite images taken in 2017 show some of the buildings remaining, but from road level only ruins are visible.

Custer was apparently annoyed by the short distances covered on the previous two days' marches. On May 24 he pushed the men and animals nineteen miles. Still believing the Indians were concentrated on the Little Missouri River, he was anxious to engage the enemy.

Green River is a modern name. Terry and others simply recorded the waterbody as a branch of the Heart, or Big Heart, River. They also noted this camp was located approximately one and a half miles north of Stanley's Crossing, used by Colonel David Stanley during the Yellowstone Expedition of 1873. Custer was second-in-command under Stanley, and many officers and enlisted men of the 7th Cavalry were veterans of the earlier campaign.

Custer Camp
#8

Figure 25. Custer Camp #8 as seen from the Green River Bridge on I-94 West. (photo location: GPS 46.879335, -102.608861, facing north)

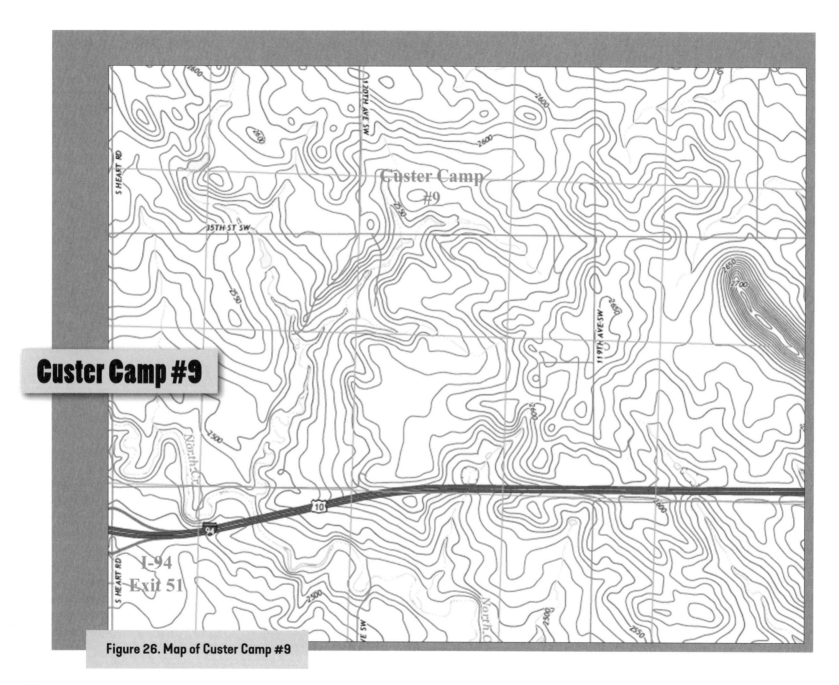

Custer Camp #9

Figure 26. Map of Custer Camp #9

Custer Camp #9

May 25, 1876

General Location: 3.0 miles north of South Heart, North Dakota

Ownership Status: private property but visible from public road

GPS Coordinates: 46.907534, -102.973429

Directions:

1. From I-94 West, take Exit 51 to South Heart Road.

2. Turn north (right) onto South Heart Road and go 1.1 miles to 35th Street SW.

3. Turn east (right) onto 35th St SW and go 1.2 miles. Custer's camp was on the hillside just north (left) of the road.

Another long march of almost twenty miles brought the Dakota Column to this camp. It was situated at the headwaters of what today is named North Creek, another tributary to the Heart River. Journal entries from Terry and Lieutenant Edward Godfrey say little about the camp. Godfrey mentioned only that they camped "beside wood and water" on a fork of the Heart River.

Custer Camp #9

Figure 27. Custer Camp #9 was along a small, often dry, tributary to what is now called North Creek. (photo location: GPS 46.905275, -102.976570, facing east along 35th Street SW)

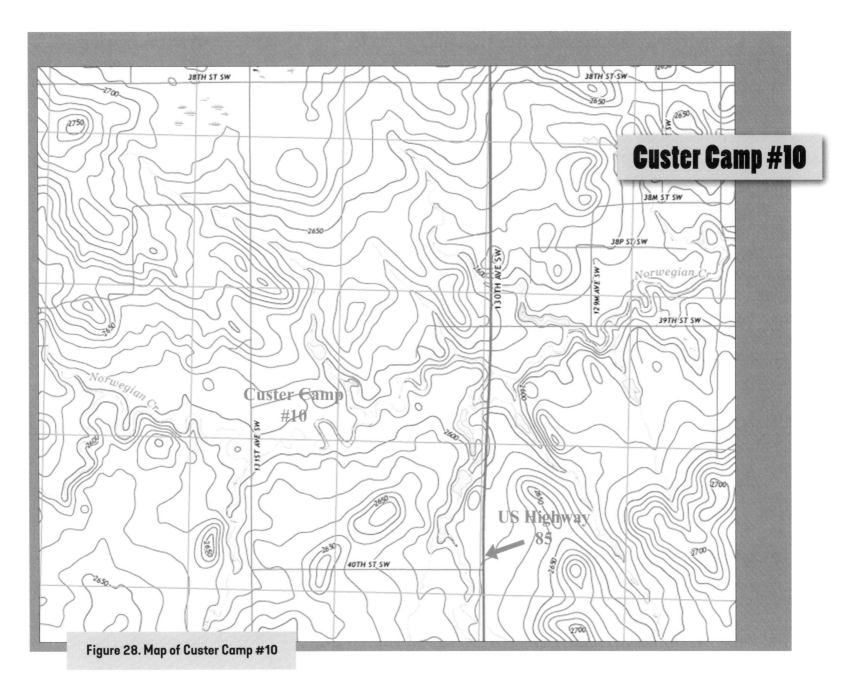

Figure 28. Map of Custer Camp #10

Custer Camp #10

May 26, 1876

General Location: 3.0 miles south of Belfield, North Dakota

Ownership Status: private property but visible from public road

GPS Coordinates: 46.843463, -103.207403

Directions:

1. From I-94 West, take Exit 42 (at Belfield) to US Highway 85.

2. Turn south (left) onto US 85 and go 4.5 miles, through Belfield, to 40th Street SW.

3. Turn west (right) onto 40th Street SW and go 1.0 miles to 131st Avenue SW.

4. Turn north (right) onto 131st Avenue SW and go 0.7 miles. Custer's tenth camp was located east of the road. An oilfield waste disposal facility now occupies the site.

Custer's tenth campsite was located along Norwegian Creek, but like earlier sites it was known at the time as merely a branch of the Heart River. Unlike the previous camp, however, wood was scarce here. Several bridges had to be constructed during the day's march. This meant using timbers that were brought on the wagons from Fort Abraham Lincoln rather than relying on wood found along the streams. The tenth camp was the column's last camp before they descended into the badlands. It was noted that cactus was becoming more common.

Custer Camp #10

Figure 29. Custer's tenth campsite is now occupied by an oilfield waste disposal facility. (photo location: GPS 46.832600, -103.204365, facing north)

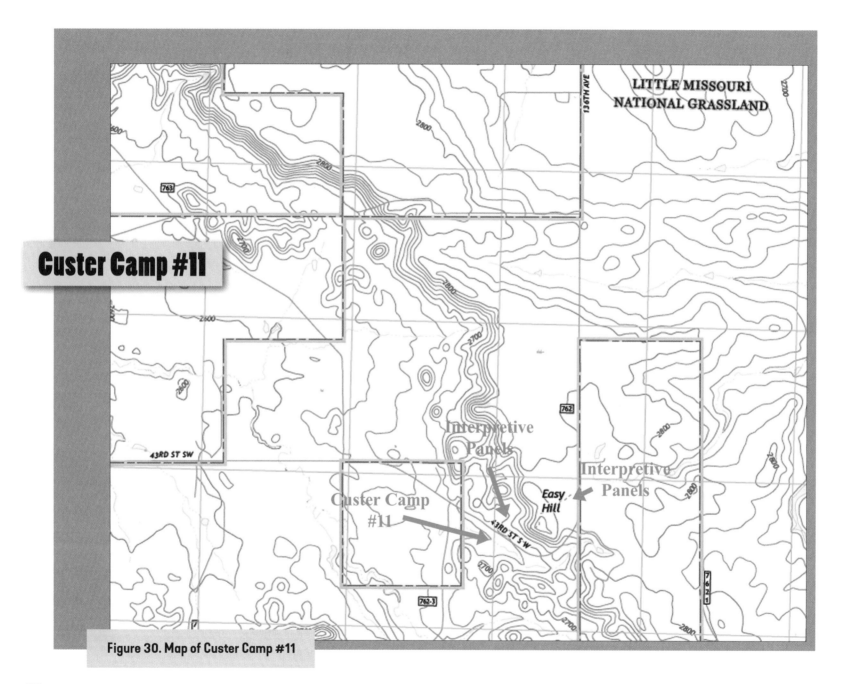

Figure 30. Map of Custer Camp #11

Custer Camp #11

May 27, 1876

General Location: 6.0 miles south of Fryburg, North Dakota

Ownership Status:
mix of private and public property but is visible from public road

GPS Coordinates: 46.785119, -103.325236

Directions:

1. From I-94 West, take Exit 36 to Main Street.

2. Turn south (left) onto Main Street and follow it 2.5 miles through Fryburg to Sully Creek Road.

3. Turn west (right) onto Sully Creek Road and go 0.6 miles to 136th Avenue.

4. Turn south (left) onto 136th Avenue and go 5.1 miles to the parking lot at the Easy Hill interpretive panels.

5. After Easy Hill, 136th Avenue begins to turn west (right) and to descend into the badlands. Continue past the Easy Hill parking lot for 0.7 miles to another interpretive area. Note that the road is now called 43rd Street SW. The parking lot and interpretive panels for Custer's eleventh campsite are on the north (right) side of the road. The Dakota Column camped along Davis Creek on the south (left) side of the road.

The actual location of Custer's eleventh camp is uncertain. On older topographic maps, the flat land above and immediately east of the entrance into the badlands at Davis Creek is labeled "Custer's Campsite." This label is either incorrect or it possibly refers to a campsite from one of his previous expeditions through the area. Chorne stated the camp was located within the northwest quarter of Section 9, Township 138, Range 100. This location corresponds to the label on the older maps. Anders, however, placed the camp within Section 8 of the same Township and Range. The current US Forest Service interpretive panels are located in Section 8 within the badlands and Davis Creek Canyon. Based on various journal entries, I believe this is the correct location. According to Lieutenant Godfrey, "We went down Davis Creek and camped about two miles from the entrance to the Bad Lands."[13] Terry said only, "Encamped in valley of [Davis] Creek."[14] Mark Kellogg, the reporter for the *Bismarck Tribune*, went into further detail: "Marched ten miles, and struck entrance of Bad Lands & went into camp, grass on a feeder the head of Davis Creek. Grass excellent. Water slightly alkalized, Valley narrow, camp stretches out lengthwise & it is the most picturesque imaginable. Red, cone topped Buttes in all directions."[15] Based on these three journals alone, it seems obvious that the eleventh camp was in the valley, not above it as Chorne suggested.

While guiding the column from the tenth to the eleventh camp, Custer missed the turn into Davis Creek Canyon and continued marching another four miles south before the mistake was realized. He apparently had no regard for the extra miles the infantry and unmounted cavalry had to walk, but General Terry was not happy

---

[13]Edward Settle Godfrey, *The Godfrey Diary of the Battle of the Little Bighorn*, Big Byte Books, Kindle Edition 2014.

[14] Alfred H. Terry, The Terry Diary.

[15]Mark Kellogg Diary, available at https://www.history.nd.gov/archives/Kelloggdiary.pdf

about the detour. Most officers at the time likely cared nothing about the plight of the enlisted soldier, but Terry seemed to sympathize somewhat with their hardships.

As the troops were moving into camp, they were serenaded by the regimental band. Jacob Horner, a Private in the 7th Cavalry, recalled that "General Custer had the band get up on the sides of the buttes and play music while the camp was being made and the animals taken care of."[16]

Although the campsite can be seen from the roadway, the best view of the site and the surrounding badlands can be found from the top of Easy Hill. A trail a quarter of a mile each way leads from the Easy Hill parking area to an overlook on Easy Hill's summit. The trail is marked with a couple of wooden posts and the section nearest the parking area is mowed from time to time. Once you start the climb up the actual hill, the trail is easily discernable.

---

[16]Usher L. Burdick and Eugene D. Hart, *Jacob Horner and the Indian Campaigns of 1876 and 1877: The Sioux and Nez Perce* (Baltimore: Wirth Brothers, 1942).

Pass into Davis Creek Canyon

Easy Hill

Figure 31. Easy Hill and the entrance to the badlands via Davis Creek Canyon, as seen from the Easy Hill parking area. (photo location: GPS 46.787245, -103.316054 facing west)

Custer Camp
#11

Figure 32. Custer Camp #11 as seen from 43rd Street SW.
(photo location: GPS 46.785442, -103.324034, facing southwest)

Custer Camp #11

Figure 33. Custer Camp #11 as viewed from atop Easy Hill. (photo location: GPS 46.785075, -103.319528, facing southwest)

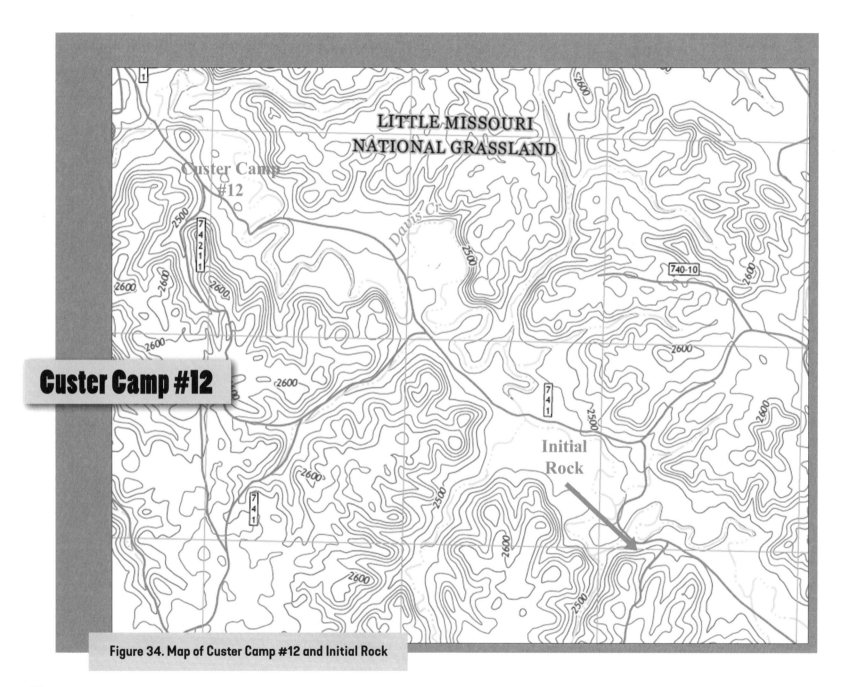

Figure 34. Map of Custer Camp #12 and Initial Rock

Custer Camp #12

May 28, 1876

General Location: 7.5 miles southeast of Medora, North Dakota

Ownership Status: public (Little Missouri National Grassland)

GPS Coordinates: 46.823880, -103.439185

Directions:

1. From the parking lot of the interpretive area near Custer Camp #11, continue west on 43rd Street SW for 2.5 miles to Forest Road 740.

2. Veer northwest (right) onto FR 740 and go 2.3 miles to the parking lot at the Initial Rock interpretive area. Park here.

3. If conditions permit, cross Davis Creek just west of the parking lot and hike 2.2 miles to the site of Custer's twelfth camp. Note that Davis Creek will have to be crossed at least three more times on the walk.

As the soldiers marched down Davis Creek, they had to deal with multiple stream crossings. Fortunately, the Dakota Column had the luxury of men and materials to build temporary bridges whereas the modern visitor does not. At one such crossing, guards were placed on nearby rocks to provide cover for the bridge builders. Two guards, Privates Frank Neely and William Williams, apparently grew bored with the extra duty and decided to carve their names into the sandstone. The carvings still exist and are protected by the US Forest Service. Except for some very faint wagon ruts at a few locations, Initial Rock is the only physical evidence that remains of the Dakota Column's march to the Little Bighorn.

Private Neely and Private Williams both survived the battle at the Little Bighorn a month later. Both were in Captain Benteen's battalion on Reno Hill. Private Neely spent twelve years in the army before being discharged. While still on duty, he accidentally killed another man. One of his fellow troopers recalled that he was greatly affected by the incident. Soon after he was discharged, he wandered off and was never seen again. Private Williams was discharged two years after the battle. He eventually became a druggist.

Theoretically, this should be an easy campsite to reach if you don't mind a hike. However, as the Dakota Column learned in 1876, traveling along Davis Creek can be difficult following periods of heavy rain. Although Davis Creek is only about ten to fifteen feet wide, the stream bed consists of clay. It has the consistency of the slurry used on a potter's wheel and is extremely difficult to cross on foot. I made two attempts, first in June 2018 and again in September 2019. I failed on both occasions.

After my second try, I decided to approach the camp from the high ground to the north. You won't be able to stand on the site by this route, but at least you'll be able to see it. Some words of caution, however, before you attempt this trek:

- This is remote country. Do not try this route unless you are completely skilled with the use of GPS devices, topographic maps, and a compass. While some of the route is along discernable trails, much is not.
- Rattlesnakes are supposedly very common in the area. I personally didn't see any on my hike, but it's usually the one you don't see that gets you. Wear appropriate boots.
- Carry plenty of water. It's not a particularly long hike—about two miles each way—but the climate here is typically hot, dry, and windy. Dehydration occurs much quicker than most people realize.
- Do not hike this alone. Cell phone service is spotty. If you get hurt, your hiking partner may be able to lead rescuers to you.
- As you hike toward the vantage point, turn around from time to time and make mental notes of the route behind you. This will make the return trip easier. Of course, you should also be using your GPS device to create a track that you can follow back to your starting point.
- And finally, when you arrive at the overlook, do not get too close to the edge. These are not granite cliffs. They are brittle sandstone outcroppings. Watch your footing.

So, if you absolutely have to see Custer's twelfth campsite, this is the route I followed. Don't say you weren't warned:

1) From Initial Rock, backtrack out of the canyon up to Easy Hill and then go north on 136th Avenue until it dead ends at Sully Creek Road.
2) Turn left (west) onto Sully Creek Road and go 7.1 miles to Forest Service Road 740.
3) Turn left (south) onto Forest Service Road 740. Although signs say this is a private road, it is in fact a Forest Service road with public access. A private mining company, however, maintains it. Follow this road for 1.0 miles until it makes a sharp turn to the left (east). From this point, FS 740 continues straight (south) as a smaller double track trail.
4) Continue south on FS 740 for another 0.25 miles until you come to a barbed-wire gate. If closed, open the gate and drive through, closing the gate behind you. Remember, this is open range. If the gate is already open, leave it the way you find it.
5) After passing through the gate, continue south on this double track trail for another 0.4 miles until you come to a fork in the road. Drive no further.
6) You are now at the start of the hike (GPS 46.841150, -103.423469). I'll call this "Waypoint 1," and it is marked as "1" on Figure 39, page 56.
7) One fork takes off to the left, but you need to continue straight and proceed slightly downhill for approximately 0.25 miles to another fork in the trail (GPS 46.837708, -103.421924). You are now at Waypoint 2.
8) At this fork, veer right and continue downhill for another 0.15 miles to a small, intermittent stream (GPS 46.835448, -103.422632). This is Waypoint 3.
9) Cross the stream and continue uphill for 0.1 miles until you are between a small pond on your right and an old hay shed on your left (GPS 46.833929, -103.422927). This is Waypoint 4.
10) Continue southward and uphill on the trail for another 0.3 miles. Stop here. This is where you will leave the trail (GPS 46.829693, -103.421366). This is Waypoint 5.
11) Turn right (west). You will see a rocky ridge ahead of you. Climb to the top of it. It's a climb of about 50 feet and is moderately steep (GPS 46.829590, -103.422761). You're now at Waypoint 6.

12) As you descend from the ridge, you'll see a deep draw in front of you. Veer to the left and follow the base of the ridge to avoid the thick vegetation in the draw. Continue along the base of the ridge until you reach the top of the draw and can step across (GPS 46.827469, -103.421881). This is Waypoint 7.

13) Once on the opposite side of the draw, veer back to the right and follow along the base of that ridge, staying out of the draw to avoid the vegetation. After approximately 0.1 miles, you'll come to the point of the ridge and what appears to be a small pit (GPS 46.828148, -103.423721). This is Waypoint 8.

14) Circle to the left around the point and you'll notice a cove. Cut straight across the mouth of the cove to the opposite point. Here you will find a barbed wire fence that starts at the base of the bluff. There is no gate. The best way to cross a barbed wire fence is to slide under it on your back so you can see the wire above you (GPS 46.826750, -103.424617). This is Waypoint 9.

15) Once you're on the other side of the wire, you'll see a gap and another bluff to your left. Pass to the right side of that bluff (GPS 46.826618, -103.426012). You're at Waypoint 10.

16) From this point onward, you'll basically be hiking along the top of a broad ridge. Go 0.2 miles to what looks like a meadow. You'll have to maneuver around some piles of rocks and small knolls (GPS 46.826202, -103.429208). This is Waypoint 11.

17) Continue another 0.1 miles in the same basic direction to a saddle between two small knolls (GPS 46.825700, -103.430722). This is Waypoint 12.

18) Finally, walk in the same general direction for another 0.2 miles until you reach the Vantage Point (GPS 46.824635, -103.435314) to see Custer's twelfth campsite in the valley below.

Figure 35. Initial Rock is protected and interpreted by the US Forest Service. It is located along Forest Service Road 740 between Custer's eleventh and twelfth campsites. (photo location: GPS 46.807678, -103.411699, facing east)

Figure 36. Carving made by Private Frank Neely of "M" Company, 7th Cavalry. (photo location: GPS 46.807500, -103.411100, Initial Rock)

Figure 37. Carving made by Private William Williams of "H" Company, 7th Cavalry. (photo location: GPS , 46.807500, -103.411100, Initial Rock)

Figure 38. This is the view down Davis Creek Canyon from Initial Rock. Custer's twelfth campsite was located approximately one and a half miles ahead. (photo location: GPS 46.807500, -103.411100, facing west)

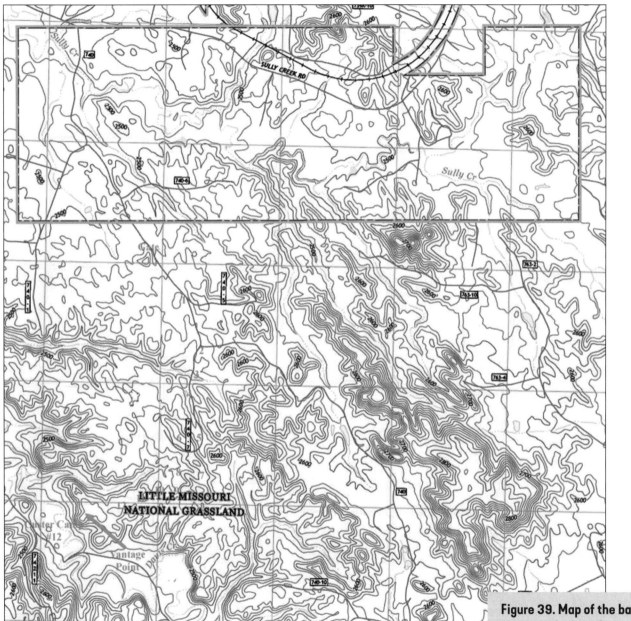

Figure 39. Map of the backcountry route to a vantage point overlooking Custer's twelfth campsite.

Davis Creek

Custer Camp #12

Figure 40. Custer Camp #12 as seen from a vantage point on the north rim of Davis Creek Canyon. (photo location: GPS 46.824635, -103.435314, facing southwest down into the canyon)

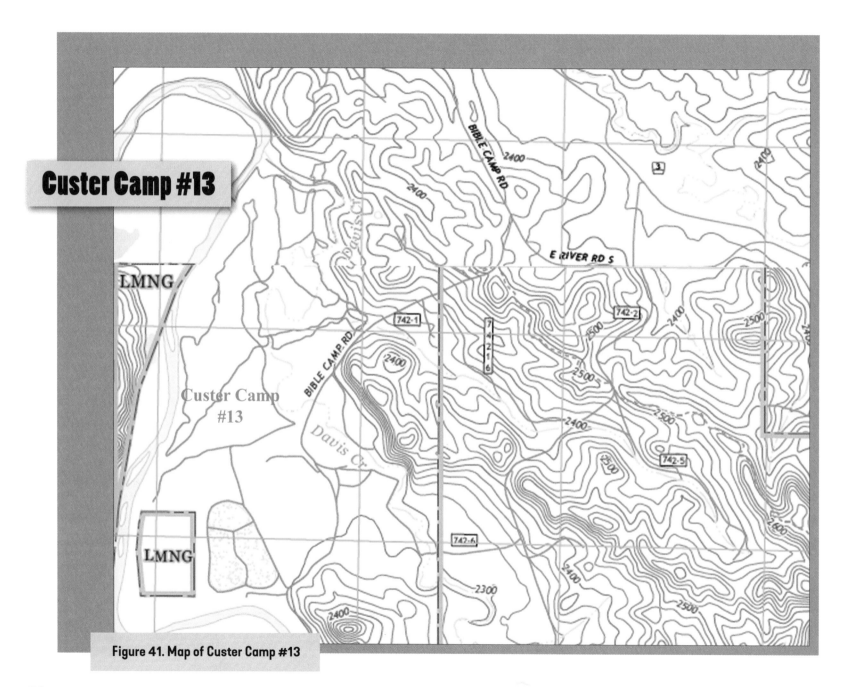

Custer Camp #13

Figure 41. Map of Custer Camp #13

Custer Camp #13

May 29–30, 1876

General Location: 3.3 miles south of Medora, North Dakota

Ownership Status:
private property but open to the public (Bully Pulpit Golf Course)

GPS Coordinates: 46.867402, -103.539275

Directions:

1. From I-94 West, take Exit 27.

2. Exit 27 merges into Pacific Avenue. Follow Pacific Avenue 1.4 miles to East River Road South in Medora.

3. urn west (left) onto East River Road South and go 2.9 miles to Bible Camp Road.

4. Turn west (right) onto Bible Camp Road and go 0.9 miles to the Bully Pulpit Golf Course. Custer's thirteenth camp was located where the golf course is now situated.

When the Dakota Column came to the mouth of Davis Creek, they set up camp on the east side of the Little Missouri River. Until now, all the previous camps had been occupied for a single night. Here they spent two nights.

From the time the troops left Fort Abraham Lincoln, they expected to find and engage the Indians near the Little Missouri. They were surprised and disappointed when they arrived at the river and found no recent signs of the Sioux or their Cheyenne allies. Not that they were disappointed by the lack of an enemy, but now all realized the campaign was going to last much longer than they had hoped.

Friction between Terry and Custer was mounting. Terry was displeased with Custer's lack of sympathy for the troops, and Custer was growing weary of Terry's oversight and cautiousness. Custer asked Terry for permission to lead a scouting expedition south along the river. Terry agreed to a day's delay so Custer could make his reconnaissance. No doubt he felt Custer's absence from the column would be a welcomed break for himself and the rest of the troops.

On the morning of May 30, Custer headed south with his four favorite companies of cavalry. In total, approximately 250 men accompanied him. They rode twenty miles south, ate lunch, and then returned to camp around 6:00 p.m. Many soldiers felt the entire scout was nothing more than a joyride for Custer and his close circle of loyal officers.

Custer Camp #13

Figure 42. Custer Camp #13 as seen from the deck of the Bully Pulpit Golf Course Clubhouse. (photo location: GPS 46.873235, -103.530401, facing southwest)

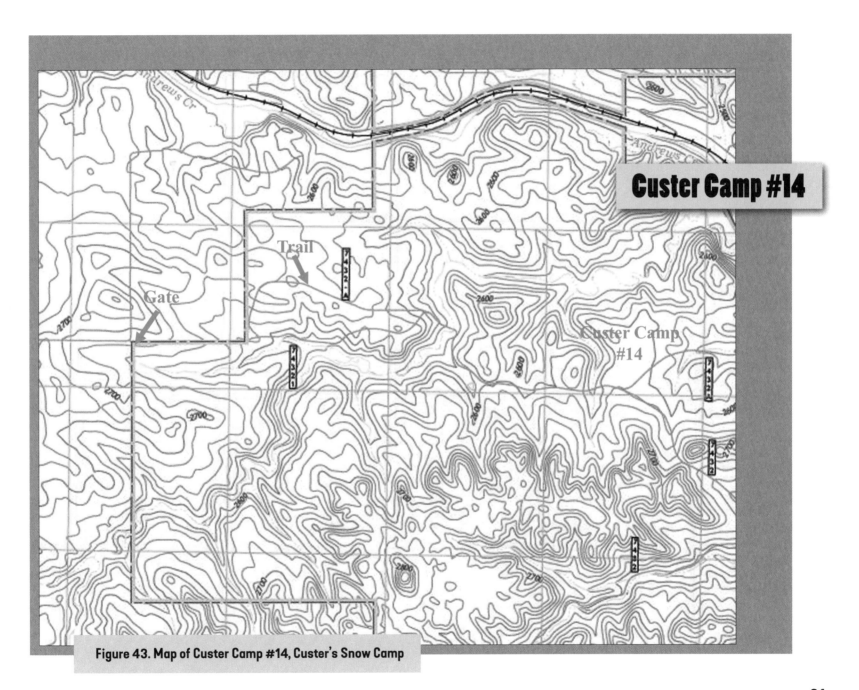

Custer Camp #14

Trail

Gate

Custer Camp #14

Figure 43. Map of Custer Camp #14, Custer's Snow Camp

Custer Camp #14

May 31–June 2, 1876

General Location: 7.8 miles west of Medora, North Dakota

Ownership Status: public (Little Missouri National Grassland)

GPS Coordinates: 46.903897, -103.692283

Directions:

1. From Medora, take I-94 West to Exit 10.

2. Turn south (left) onto County Road 11 and go 2.1 miles to the town of Sentinel Butte.

3. Continue south on CR 11 for another mile until it makes a sharp turn to the east (left) and becomes 35th Street SW.

4. Go east on 35th SW for 5.0 miles until it dead ends at a large metal gate. This is the western boundary of the Little Missouri National Grassland. You can park at the gate and walk in or if conditions permit you can open the gate and drive in. Make sure to close the gate behind you.

5. At the gate, the road becomes a double track trail. If driving, continue on this trail for 1.2 miles until it starts to descend into a deep draw. Park here. Do not drive into the draw. Note that a smaller trail connects to the main trail along the way. Stay on the main trail for the easiest route, but both trails rejoin prior to entering the draw.

6. Continue walking along the main trail for another 1.1 miles. You'll come to a broad plateau with a large, high-voltage power line to the south and a smaller power line to the north. The smaller power line runs right across the middle of the Dakota Column's fourteenth camp.

This campsite is the third of three that are not easily viewed from a road. It requires a round trip hike of two to four miles across open range, depending on where you park. The hike is relatively easy hike for anyone of moderate physical condition, with no steep hills to climb and only one small creek to step across. The trail is distinct, but it is always best to have a map, compass, and GPS device. Cell service along the route is spotty. Carry water and be on the lookout for rattlesnakes.

Custer's fourteenth camp is often referred to as his "Snow Camp." On the morning of May 31, the men of the Dakota Column woke to cold and dreary conditions. Tents were wet and the damp wood meant no fires for cooking. For most, breakfast consisted of hardtack and raw bacon. The crossing of the Little Missouri was easy enough; bridges had been constructed on the previous day. The climb out of the valley, however, was torturous. Less than eight miles were covered in the day's march. At around 2:00 p.m. the column halted and established camp. Later that evening, the rain intensified.

When reveille sounded on the morning of June 1, the troops found the ground covered with two-to-three inches of snow. Orders came down that camp would not be broken until further notice. Snow continued to fall throughout the day. In fact, the blizzard did not end until midday on June 2. When the snow stopped falling, the accumulation on the ground melted rapidly, leaving the soldiers and livestock to deal with cold, sticky mud. They remained in place for one more night.

**Custer Camp
#14**

Figure 44. Custer's fourteenth campsite, his Snow Camp, was located on this broad, flat plateau. The power pole in the center of the photograph is located at the approximate center of the camp. (photo location: GPS 46.902871, -103.693471, facing north)

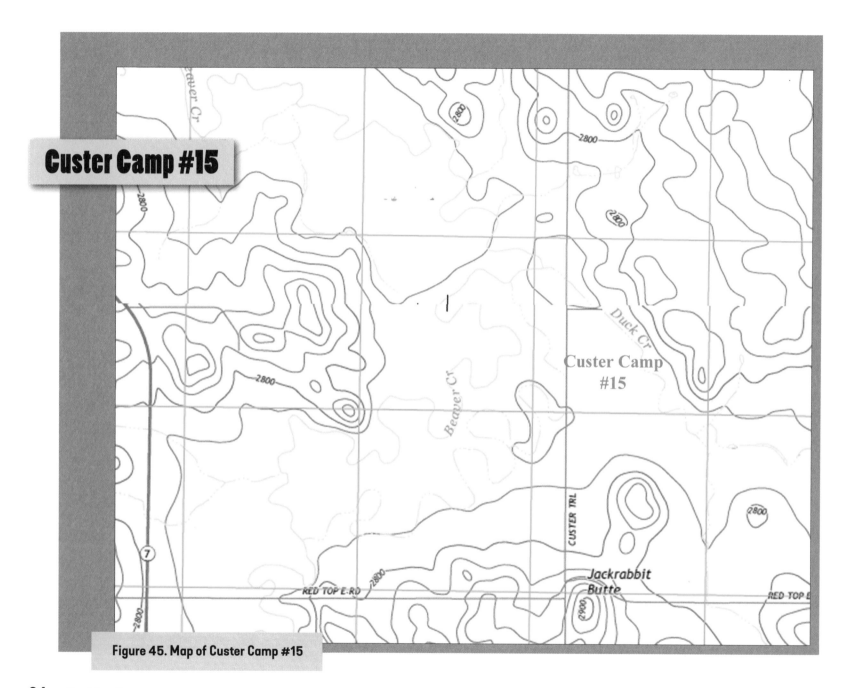

Custer Camp #15

Custer Camp #15

Figure 45. Map of Custer Camp #15

Custer Camp #15

June 3, 1876

General Location: 8.0 miles south of Wibaux, Montana

Ownership Status: private property but visible from public road

GPS Coordinates: 46.876351, –104.157597

Directions:

1. From I-94 West, take Exit 242 at Wibaux, Montana, to Montana Highway 7.

2. Turn south (left) onto MT 7 and follow it 9.9 miles to Red Top East Road.

3. Turn east (left) onto Red Top East Road and go 1.5 miles to Custer Trail.

4. Turn north (left) onto Custer Trail and go 1.1 miles. Custer camped here at the junction of Beaver Creek and Duck Creek.

Departing the Snow Camp shortly after 5:00 a.m., Terry's intention was to march west towards Stanley's Stockade near present day Glendive, Montana. Stanley's Stockade, if you recall, was the supply depot on the Yellowstone River established by Colonel David Stanley during his 1873 Yellowstone Expedition. Five hours into the march, eastbound riders were seen on the horizon. These three men turned out to be couriers from the stockade. Terry was informed there were no Indians between his current position and the Yellowstone River. He also learned Colonel Gibbon and his Montana Column had found signs of a large concentration of Indians south of the Yellowstone in the vicinity of Rosebud Creek.

With this new information, Terry changed his plan, something he apparently hated to do. He sent orders back to Stanley's Stockade telling Gibbon to hold his position at the Rosebud and instructing one boatload of supplies to be moved up the Yellowstone to the mouth of the Powder River. Terry's revised plan was to move south along Beaver Creek, turn west across the divide to O'Fallon Creek, and then follow that creek downstream (north) to its confluence with the Yellowstone.

After a march of twenty-five miles, their longest march so far, the Dakota Column halted at 4:30 p.m. They set up camp on the east side of Beaver Creek at the junction of Duck Creek.

Custer Camp #15

Figure 46. Custer Camp #15 as seen from near the intersection of Custer Trail and Red Top East Road. (photo location: GPS 46.861189, -104.156742, facing north)

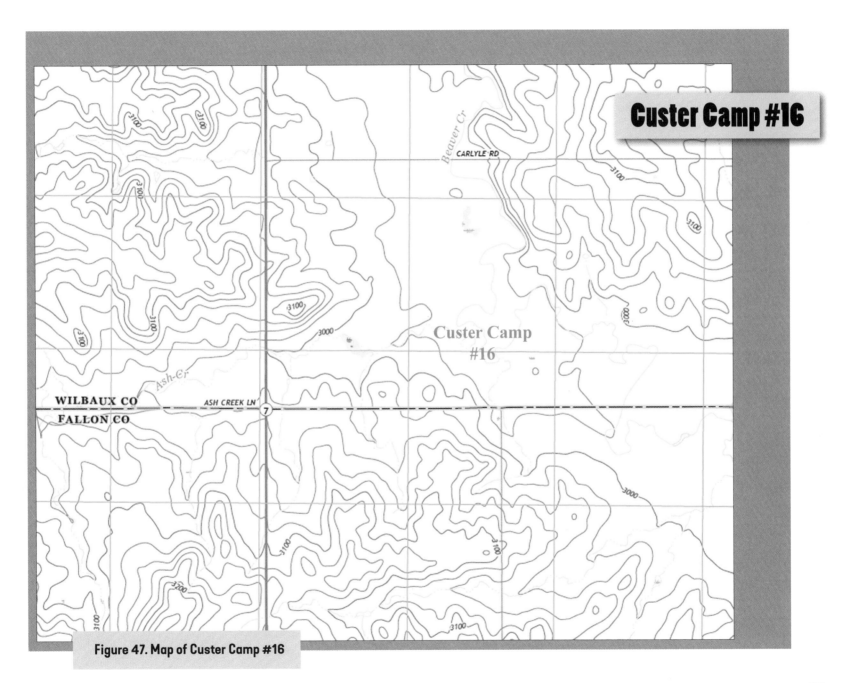

Custer Camp #16

Figure 47. Map of Custer Camp #16

Custer Camp #16

June 4, 1876

General Location: 19.3 miles north of Baker, Montana

Ownership Status: private property but visible from public road

GPS Coordinates: 46.644618, -104.211154

Directions:

1. From US Highway 12 in Baker, Montana, follow MT 7 north 19.2 miles to Ash Creek Road.

2. Turn east (right) onto Ash Creek Road and go 1.0 miles. Custer's sixteenth camp was on the west side Beaver Creek just north (left) of the road.

Camp #16 was located where a small intermittent stream called Ash Creek joined Beaver Creek from the west. The site was previously used by Colonel Stanley's expedition in 1873 and was, therefore, familiar to Custer and many of his men. During the day's march, the column crossed from the east side to the west side of Beaver Creek. The day was very hot and General Terry suffered with what was believed to be heat stroke. He rode part of the way in a wagon.

Custer Camp #16

Figure 48. Custer's sixteenth camp was located at the confluence of two small streams, Beaver Creek and Ash Creek. (photo location: GPS 46.641378, -104.209743, facing north)

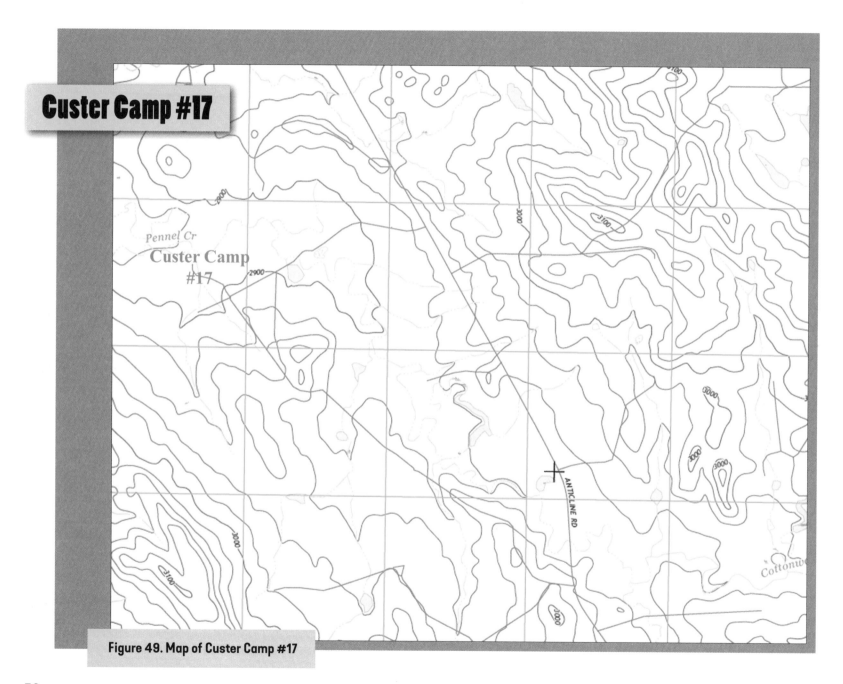

Figure 49. Map of Custer Camp #17

Custer Camp #17

June 5, 1876

General Location: 8.2 miles northwest of Baker, Montana

Ownership Status: private property but visible from public road

GPS Coordinates: 46.470499, -104.362341

Directions:

1. From US Highway 12 in Baker, take Montana Highway 7 north 1.0 miles to Pennel Road.

2. Turn west (left) onto Pennel Road and follow it 4.9 miles to Anticline Road. Note that Pennel Road makes several jogs to the north and west along this course.

3. Veer north (right) onto Anticline Road and go 3.5 miles. At this point, face west (left). The site of Custer's seventeenth camp will be directly in front of you on the opposite side of Pennel Creek.

From their camp on Beaver Creek, the column continued south another ten miles before turning westward. As they left the valley of Beaver Creek, the environment changed drastically. Instead of fresh water and luxurious grass, they now entered a landscape dominated by "sagebrush, cactus, and rattlesnakes," according to Mark Kellogg.[17] They crossed Pennel Creek and traveled up the west bank about two miles before setting up camp. In total, the day's march was just over twenty miles.

---

[17]Mark Kellogg, Diary

Custer Camp #17

Figure 50. Custer Camp #17. The few trees in this photograph mark the approximate course of Pennel Creek. (photo location: GPS 46.471502, -104.347903, facing southwest)

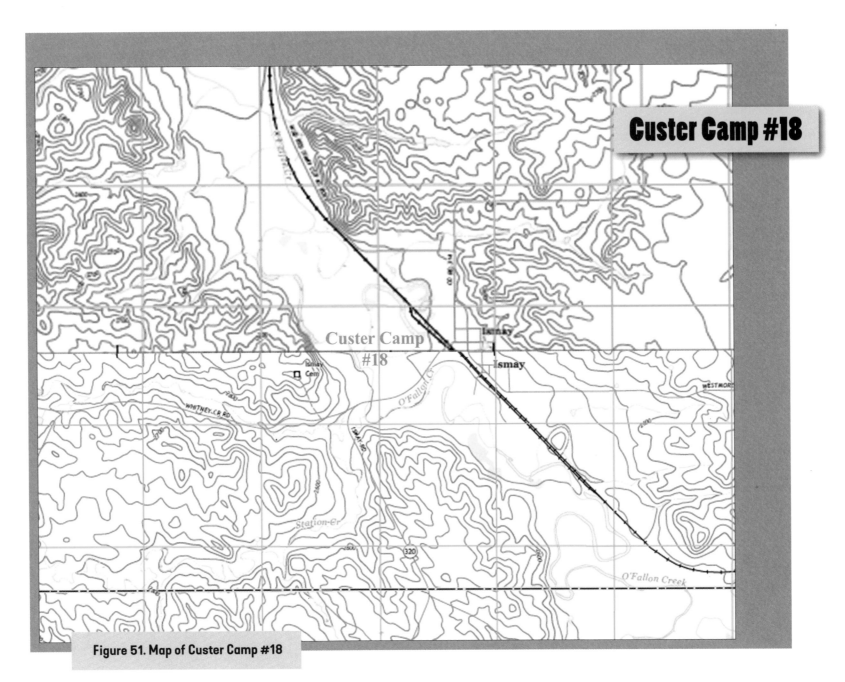

Custer Camp #18

Custer Camp
#18

Figure 51. Map of Custer Camp #18

Custer Camp #18

June 6, 1876

General Location: 0.7 miles west of Ismay, Montana

Ownership Status: private property but visible from public road

GPS Coordinates: 46.498758, -104.807402

Directions:

1. From Baker, take US Highway 12 west 25.2 miles to Ismay Road.

2. Turn north (right) onto Ismay Road and follow it 5.4 miles to the bridge over O'Fallon Creek. Custer's eighteenth camp was on the west bank of O'Fallon Creek just north of the bridge.

From their camp on Pennel Creek, the Dakota Column headed in a general westerly direction until striking what they referred to as the headwaters of O'Fallon Creek (probably now Sandstone Creek, a tributary to O'Fallon Creek). The intention was to follow it northwest until they reached the Yellowstone River. Somehow their guides, led by Charley Reynolds, got confused. Instead of staying along the main course of the creek, they directed the column upstream and southwest along another tributary. As Terry recorded in his journal, "Halted to water in branch of O'Fallons 12.20. Discovered at this point that the guides had led us astray." By the time the mistake was realized, the column had deviated nine miles from the planned route. The resulting eighteen-mile detour irritated Terry considerably. It was around 4:30 p.m. before camp was finally established.

During the day, the column had managed to cross to the west side of O'Fallon Creek. This was fortuitous. Overnight a severe thunderstorm struck. By the next morning, O'Fallon Creek was swollen beyond its banks. Crossing under those conditions would have been dangerous if not impossible.

Two other significant events occurred overnight. First, one of the troops accidentally shot himself in the leg. The injury was not fatal, but it did prevent him from participating in the battle alongside the rest of his comrades. Second, Terry, after consulting with Custer and Major Reno, decided to continue the march westward to the Powder River rather than heading straight to the Yellowstone.

Custer Camp
#18

Figure 52. Custer's eighteenth camp was located just west of Ismay, Montana, along the west bank of O'Fallon Creek. (photo location: GPS 46.496012, -104.806315, facing north)

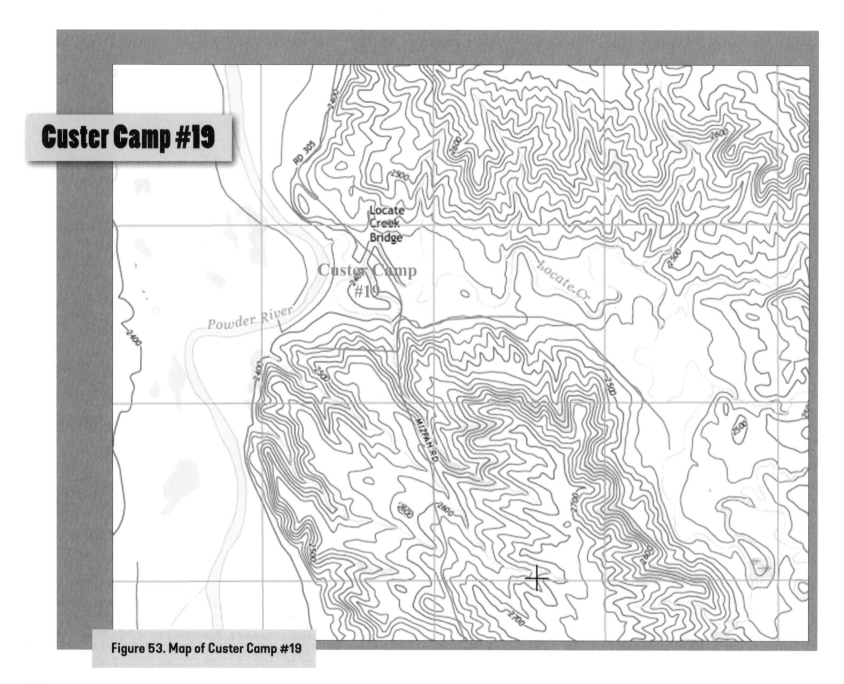

Custer Camp #19

Figure 53. Map of Custer Camp #19

Custer Camp #19

June 7–10, 1876

General Location: 22.0 miles south of Terry, Montana

Ownership Status: private property but visible from public road

GPS Coordinates: 46.473220, -105.305568

Directions:

1. From Baker, follow US Highway 12 west 50.4 miles to County Road 305 (Mizpah Road). This road is located 0.4 miles east of the Powder River Bridge.

2. Turn north (right) onto CR 305 and go 3.1 miles to the bridge over Locate Creek. Custer's camp was situated here at the confluence of Locate Creek and Powder River.

Note: This road can become very muddy after only minimal precipitation. If it has rained within the previous twenty-four hours, proceed with caution.

The column arrived here on June 7 after their longest march yet, thirty-two miles. The terrain was very rough and soft due to the previous night's storm. The men and animals were exhausted by the time they rolled into camp. Most would remain camped here for four nights.

Several significant events were initiated from this site. As they set up camp, the men were met by a courier from Stanley's Stockade. Terry was informed that the steamer *Far West* had departed that location on June 5 and was en route to the mouth of the Powder River. Terry sent a party of his Arikara scouts back downriver to the Yellowstone to advise the *Far West* of his column's location.

Late the next morning, June 8, Terry's scouts returned from the *Far West* with more dispatches. Of particular concern to Terry was the fact that his instructions to Gibbon a few days earlier did not make it through. Now Gibbon's position was unknown. Terry decided to go downriver to the mouth of the Powder River, commandeer the *Far West*, and travel upriver on the Yellowstone until Gibbon and the Montana column could be found. Shortly after noon, Terry headed north with an escort of two companies of cavalry. Custer was now put in charge of the troops encamped on the Powder River.

Before departing, Terry issued orders for the cavalry to prepare for an eight-day scouting expedition south up the Powder, then to cross the divide west towards the Tongue River. From there they were to follow the Tongue back down to the Yellowstone. Late in the afternoon it began to rain again.

June 9 started with even more rain. Preparations continued for the scouting expedition along the Powder and the Tongue Rivers. Since it would be a mounted cavalry scout only, no wagons would be brought. All of the needed provisions were to be packed by mules. This presented an array of new problems. General Crook, moving up from Wyoming, had a well-deserved reputation for using mules. He personally preferred riding mules to horses. Custer's troops, however, had no experience with the beasts. The day was spent with the troops and the mules trying to negotiate who was really in charge.

Terry, meanwhile, boarded the *Far West*. Its captain, Grant Marsh, piloted the vessel upriver in an effort to find Colonel Gibbon. They linked up in the early afternoon. During a quick meeting, Gibbon was ordered to return upriver to the mouth of the Rosebud and await further instructions. Terry then returned to the mouth of the Powder River, rejoined his cavalry escort, and arrived back at Custer's position around 10:00 p.m.

Light rain was still falling on the morning of June 10. Terry gathered his senior officers together. He ordered Captain Benteen to turn over most of his Left Wing's rations and supplies to Major Reno's Right Wing. He then ordered Major Reno to assume command of the scouting expedition. Custer had expected to personally lead his entire regiment on the scout. He was not only upset that Reno was taking charge of the expedition, but also that Reno was taking

Custer's favorite companies. Reno and six companies of cavalry left camp around 3:30 p.m. For clarity, remember that a cavalry regiment was often divided into "wings" during a march. Each wing was then subdivided into battalions. The composition of wings and battalions were adjusted as the tactical situation dictated. The basic unit of a cavalry regiment was the company, more commonly called a "troop" in cavalry jargon. Company organization rarely changed.

By 5:00 a.m. on the morning of June 11, camp had been broken and the Dakota Column was on its way to the Yellowstone. Terry was particularly worried about the wagons. He knew how rough the route along the Powder River was, having traveled it twice already. He put Custer in charge of finding a path to the Yellowstone that the wagons could traverse. Custer succeeded, and in his typical fashion he wasted no time telling the story to others. The Dakota Column, minus Major Reno and the six cavalry companies, arrived safely at the Yellowstone River.

Powder River

Custer Camp #19

Locate Creek

Figure 54. Custer's nineteenth camp was situated at the confluence of the Powder River and Locate Creek. (photo location: GPS 46.475936, -105.305929, facing west from County Road 305)

Custer Camp #19

Locate Creek

Figure 55. Custer's nineteenth campsite is bisected today by County Road 305 (also called Mizpah Road). This is the view looking back up the valley of Locate Creek. (photo location: GPS 46.475936, -105.305929, facing east from County Road 305)

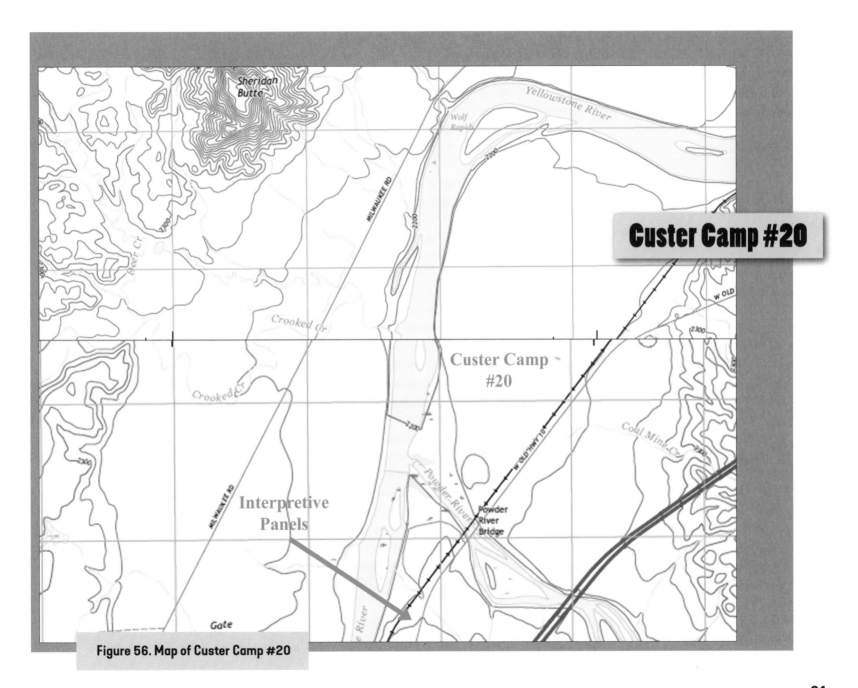

Custer Camp #20

Figure 56. Map of Custer Camp #20

Custer Camp #20

June 11–14, 1876

General Location: 6.0 miles southwest of Terry, Montana

Ownership Status:
mix of private and public property but visible from public interpretive area

GPS Coordinates: 46.752626, -105.424045

Directions:

1. From I-94 West, take Exit 169 to the unnamed access road.

2. Turn west (right) onto this access road and follow it 0.3 miles until its dead end at the Frontage Road (Old Highway 10).

3. Turn north (right) onto the Frontage Road and go 0.3 miles to the Powder River interpretive area on the left side of the road.

This camp is located on a mix of federal and state lands. A small strip of private property has to be crossed to reach the area, but an easement makes this possible. The road to the site is unmarked and primitive at best. It is basically a double-track trail and is subject to frequent flooding and washouts. The best option, however, is to view the site from the interpretive area located about a mile and a half southwest of the camp.

The Dakota Column arrived here at the junction of the Powder and Yellowstone Rivers late in the afternoon on June 11. Waiting for them was not only the steamer *Far West* but also a sutler's tent. Now, for the first time since they left Fort Abraham Lincoln, the soldiers had a place to spend their wages. Available for purchase were an assortment of canned goods, straw hats, and alcohol. As soon as camp was pitched, officers and enlisted men alike enjoyed the liquid refreshments. Military decorum being what it was at the time, the area under the sutler's tent was separated by the stock of goods. Officers made purchases on one side of the tent and enlisted men on the other. Likewise, there was no limit on the amount of alcohol an officer could buy, but the enlisted soldiers were restricted to small quantities. The Indian scouts were normally not allowed to drink any alcohol. On this occasion, however, Custer gave permission for each scout to have one drink.

The morning of June 12 was spent unloading the provisions brought up from Stanley's Stockade aboard the *Far West*. Soldiers quickly wrote letters to send with the steamer on its return voyage to the stockade for more supplies. Captain Marsh launched his vessel from the Powder River at 12:30 p.m. and, owing to the swift current of the Yellowstone, made the seventy-two-mile journey in just over three hours. The *Far West* was loaded with more supplies and then the mail was transferred to a smaller skiff to continue down the Yellowstone. Unfortunately, this boat overturned, and one soldier drowned. The mail bag was recovered. Captain Marsh did his best to dry the soaked letters by fire. One of the letters he managed to save was a letter from Custer to Libbie.

The *Far West* departed Stanley's Stockade at 3:00 a.m. on June 13 with all the remaining men and supplies that were at the camp. While the trip downriver had taken a bit over three hours, the return trip upstream took seventeen. They arrived at the mouth of the Powder River at 8:00 p.m. that evening.

General Terry decided to make this site his main supply base for the next phase of operations. The site became known as Supply Camp and later as the Powder River Depot. Terry also decided that, from this point on, only the cavalry would move forward. He and his staff would use the *Far West* as his headquarters and move upriver and downriver as necessary. The wagons, the infantry, the unmounted cavalry troops, and the Regimental Band would remain behind at the depot. The band's white horses would be brought along, but the troopers' sabers were all boxed and left behind. Besides being noisy and heavy, by 1876 sabers were primarily used in ceremonies only. They were of little value when fighting Indians. Just two cavalrymen, Lieutenants Charles DeRudio and Edward Mathey, managed to keep their sabers for the battle.

Powder River

Sheridan Butte

Yellowstone River

Custer Camp #20

Figure 57. Custer's twentieth campsite, later to be called the Powder River Depot, was established at the confluence of the Powder and Yellowstone Rivers. (photo location: GPS 46.742919, -105.430470, facing northwest)

Sheridan Butte

Custer Camp #20

Figure 58. Custer Camp #20 is best viewed from the roadside interpretive area along Old Highway 10. The camp was located just beyond the trees which line the banks of the Powder River. (photo location: GPS 46.730801, -105.434761, facing north)

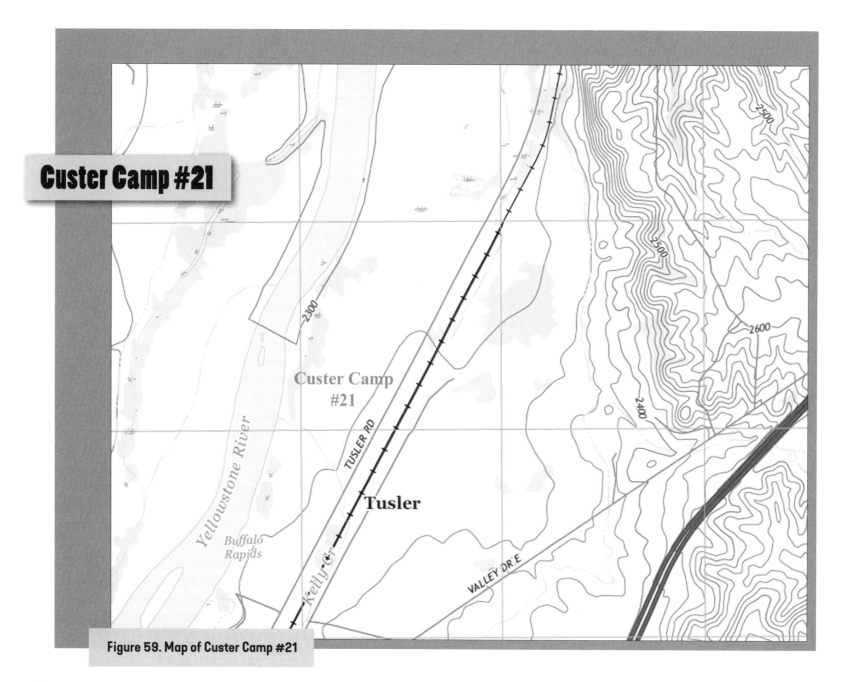

Custer Camp #21

Figure 59. Map of Custer Camp #21

Custer Camp #21

June 15, 1876

General Location: 8.9 miles northeast of Miles City, Montana

Ownership Status: private property but visible from public road

GPS Coordinates: 46.510239, -105.726705

Directions:

1. From I-94 West, take Exit 148 to Valley Drive East.

2. Turn southwest (right) onto Valley Drive East and go 1.1 miles to a dirt driveway at a business named Yellowstone Jewel. There is a sign over the driveway that reads "Camp 21." On the left side of the driveway is a sign which describes the camp.

3. After reading the sign, continue southwest on Valley Drive for another 1.4 miles to Kinsey Road.

4. Turn northwest (right) onto Kinsey Road and go 0.1 miles to Tusler Road.

5. Turn northwest (left) onto Tusler Road and drive 1.3 miles. At this point, Custer's twenty-first camp was in the tree line along the Yellowstone River to your north (left).

This is one of the few camps that are marked. The camp is on private land, but the current landowners take pride in the history of the site. The Yellowstone Jewel is a historic home that is rented for special occasions like weddings or reunions. Guests have access to trails that lead to the Yellowstone River and Custer's campsite. When facing the sign at the gate, the location of the camp is one mile directly ahead along the Yellowstone River.

Finally, after four nights encamped at the Powder River Depot, the 7th Cavalry marched away on the morning of June 15. They brought with them on their pack animals only the necessary items for subsistence. Forage, larger pieces of equipment, and supplies followed with Terry on the *Far West*.

After crossing the Powder River, Custer found the land along the south bank of the Yellowstone River to be troublesome. The ground was soft and riddled with many gullies. Although the supply wagons were left behind, one Gatling gun and its crew accompanied the cavalry. The men wheeling the gun carriage were having an extremely difficult time keeping up with the march. Custer decided to veer onto the high bluffs to the south in order to be on firmer ground. They were heading for the mouth of the Tongue River to link up with Major Reno's Right Wing. Reno was not expected to be at the Yellowstone River for a few more days, so Custer, with Captain Benteen's Left Wing, traveled at a leisurely pace.

In 1876 General George Armstrong Custer and the Seventh Cavalry, numbering several hundred soldiers camped on this property ten days before the Battle of Little Bighorn near Hardin, Montana. General Custer chose his 21st camp along the Yellowstone River and on the fields below.

WELCOME TO CAMP 21

www.yellowstonejewel.com
406-934-1122

Figure 60. A sign marks Camp #21 at the entrance to the Yellowstone Jewel along Valley Drive East. (photo location: GPS 46.507185, -105.709861, facing northwest)

Custer Camp
#21

Figure 61. Custer Camp #21 as seen from the entrance to the Yellowstone Jewel along Valley Drive East. (photo location: GPS 46.507185, -105.709861, facing northwest)

Custer Camp #21

Figure 62. A closer view of Custer Camp #21, as seen from Tusler Road. (photo location: GPS 46.512005, -105.723737, facing west)

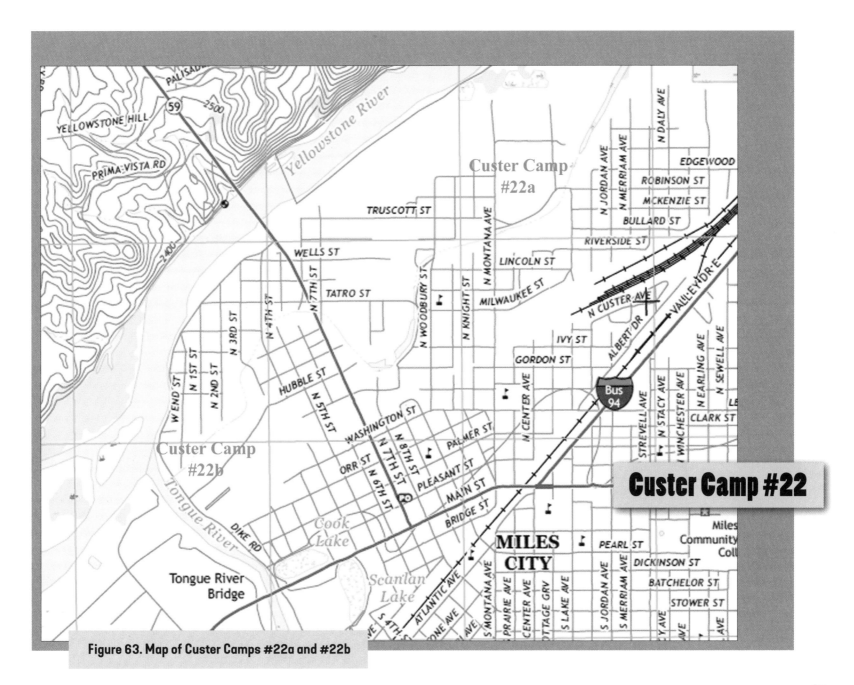

Figure 63. Map of Custer Camps #22a and #22b

Custer Camp #22

June 16–19, 1876

General Location: Miles City, Montana

Ownership Status:
Camp 22a is located in a public park. Camp 22b is situated on private land but is visible from a public road.

GPS Coordinates:
 Camp 22a: 46.423308, -105.841521
 Camp 22b: 46.409518, -105.864377

Directions:

Camp 22a:

1. From I-94 West, take Exit 138 to South Haynes Avenue.

2. Turn north (right) onto South Haynes Avenue and go 0.9 miles to Main Street.

3. Turn west (left) onto Main Street and go 1.0 miles to North Montana Avenue.

4. Turn north (right) onto North Montana Avenue and follow it 0.8 miles to Bender Park. Custer's first camp in Miles City was where Bender Park now sits.

Camp 22b:

1. From Bender Park, return south on North Montana Avenue, but go only 0.6 miles to Palmer Street.

2. Turn southwest (left) onto Palmer Street and go 0.9 miles until its dead end at Dike Road.

3. Turn northwest (right) onto Dike Road and go 0.4 miles. The mouth of the Tongue River is on the left side of the road, and Custer's second campsite in Miles City is on the right-hand side.

Custer camped near the Tongue River at two separate locations. As the troops were approaching the mouth of the Tongue River on June 16, 1876, they came upon the remnants of a Lakota camp that had been used the previous winter. There they found the bones of a soldier who had apparently been beaten to death at the camp. Clubs and sticks were on the ground near his remains. Also at the camp were the burial scaffolds of a number of Lakota. In order to examine the camp more closely, Custer ordered an early halt. Camp was then set up on the old Lakota site.

No sooner than Custer's camp was established, the pillaging and desecration of the Lakota burial scaffolds began. Officers and enlisted men alike collected trinkets and personal items from the dead. It should be noted that not all of the troops participated in the grave robbing. A number of them, as well as the Arikara scouts, were shocked by the whole affair. In most cultures, disturbing the dead is taboo even if the dead happens to be an enemy.

Early the next morning, June 17, the cavalry moved their camp the remaining two miles to the mouth of the Tongue River. They were in their new camp by 8:30 a.m. The *Far West*, which had been following close behind, entered the Tongue River and moored on the west bank about five hundred yards upstream from the Yellowstone.

For the next three days, the troops enjoyed a relatively easy time. There were, of course, the typical camp chores to be done, chores that had previously been performed by the infantry. While the officers read and played cards, the enlisted found time to bathe, wash clothes, fish, and surprisingly, collect rocks. Some of the crew of the *Far West* occupied their time panning for gold. The big question on Terry's mind, however, was the location of Reno and the Right Wing.

Terry finally got his answer on the evening of June 19. Two scouts from Reno's command arrived at the Tongue River with a note from the Major. Terry was furious to learn that Reno had disobeyed his orders and continued scouting as far west as Rosebud Creek. He was now camped eight miles west of Terry's position. General Terry sent a message back to Reno telling him to stay where he was.

Custer Camp #22a

Figure 64. The site of Custer's first camp near the Tongue River, Camp #22a, is now occupied by Bender Park in Miles City, Montana. After one night at this location, the regiment moved another two miles upstream along the Yellowstone River to the mouth of the Tongue River. (photo location: GPS 46.421785, -105.843462, facing north)

Custer Camp #22b

Figure 65. Custer's second camp, Camp #22b, in present day Miles City, Montana, was located on the east bank of the Tongue River at its confluence with the Yellowstone River. (photo location: GPS 46.409384, -105.865803, facing east)

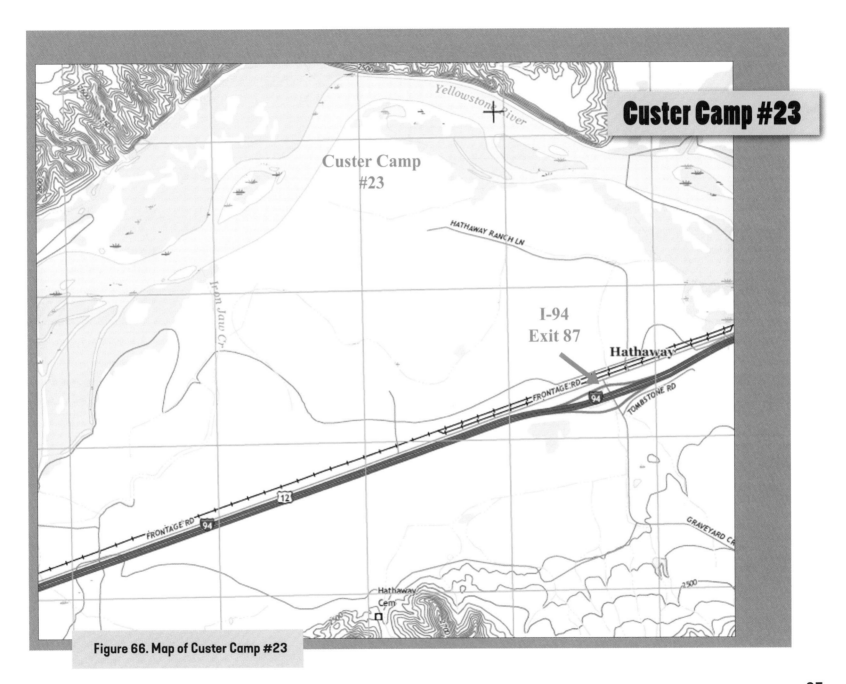

Custer Camp #23

Custer Camp
#23

I-94
Exit 87

Hathaway

Figure 66. Map of Custer Camp #23

Custer Camp #23

June 20, 1876

General Location: 1.2 miles northwest of Hathaway, Montana

Ownership Status: private property but visible from public road

GPS Coordinates: 46.288122, -106.219254

Directions:

1. From I-94 West, take Exit 117 to Graveyard Creek Road.

2. Turn north (right) onto Graveyard Creek Road and go about 150 feet to the Frontage Road.

3. Turn west (left) onto the Frontage Road and go 1.0 mile. Look north (right) of your location. One mile ahead, in the tree line along the south bank of the Yellowstone River, was Custer's twenty-third camp.

Custer was anxious to get to Reno before Terry could. Both men were mad at the Major, but for different reasons. Terry was upset that Reno had willfully disobeyed his orders and scouted all the way to the Rosebud. Custer was mad that Reno apparently found a large, fresh Indian trail and failed to follow it to their camp. Regardless of who reached him first, this would not be a great day for Major Reno.

Custer and Benteen and the Left Wing of the 7th Cavalry moved up the Tongue River from their camp until a suitable place to cross was found. After crossing, they moved to the high ground in an attempt to make better time. Meanwhile, the *Far West* moved slowly up the Yellowstone against a strong current. Both Custer and Terry arrived at Reno's position around noon, but Terry got to Reno first.

Custer and Reno boarded the *Far West* and conferred with Terry. Reno explained that no signs of recent Indian activity were found along the Powder and Tongue Rivers, but large trails were discovered leading through the valley of Rosebud Creek towards the Bighorn River. With this new information, Terry was forced to revise his battle plan again. While the meeting was taking place, supplies were being offloaded from the steamer to restock Reno's troops. Additionally, all the Gatling guns were taken onboard to free the cavalry of the burden of dragging them overland.

At the conclusion of their meeting, Terry ordered Custer to take the now reconstituted 7th Cavalry as far upstream on the Yellowstone as he could before nightfall. After another four and a half hours of marching, the column and the *Far West* settled into their camp near present-day Hathaway.

Custer Camp #23

Figure 67. Custer Camp #23 was located near the distant tree line along the Yellowstone River. (photo location: GPS 46.270978, -106.218288, facing north from the I-94 Frontage Road)

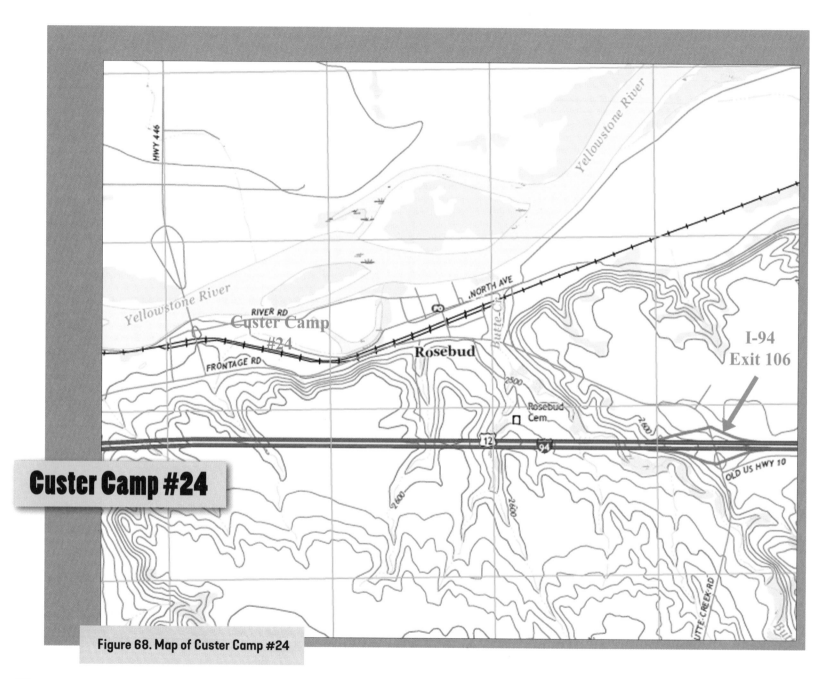

Custer Camp #24

Figure 68. Map of Custer Camp #24

Custer Camp #24

June 21, 1876

General Location: 0.7 miles west of Rosebud, Montana

Ownership Status:
private property but visible from public road

GPS Coordinates: 46.272814, -106.458176

Directions:

1. From I-94 West, take Exit 106 to Old Highway 10 (Frontage Road).

2. Turn north (right) onto Old Highway 10 and follow it 1.8 miles. At this point, Custer's twenty-fourth camp was on the north (right) side of the road, between the road and the Yellowstone River.

Terry ordered Custer to take his regiment up the Yellowstone and establish a camp near the mouth of Rosebud Creek. As the column was moving overland in that direction, the *Far West* steamed upriver to Colonel Gibbon's location. The Montana Column was camped on the north side of the Yellowstone about four miles below the Rosebud. At Gibbon's camp, the Colonel met with Terry and was instructed to have his troops move immediately to the mouth of the Bighorn River and await the arrival of the steamboat. Gibbon remained on the *Far West* with Terry, and together they continued on to the mouth of Rosebud Creek. They were there waiting for Custer as the 7th Cavalry descended the bluffs. Custer chose a campsite about three-quarters of a mile below the Rosebud's confluence with the Yellowstone. The *Far West* backtracked to Custer's location.

Soon after the *Far West* moored at Custer's camp, additional supplies were offloaded to restock the regiment. Terry called a meeting of his senior officers and staff. Custer, Gibbon, and Major Brisbin (Commander of Gibbon's 2nd Cavalry Regiment) were all present. Here the final plans were drawn up to engage the Lakota and Northern Cheyenne. Custer was ordered to take his regiment south to the head of Rosebud Creek, cross the Wolf Mountains, strike the Little Bighorn (called the Little Horn at the time), and follow it back down towards the Yellowstone. At the same time, Gibbon's troops would be ferried from the north side to the south side of the Yellowstone and proceed up the Bighorn (Big Horn) River. With luck, the enemy would be trapped between the two forces.

As preparations were underway, the sabers of Reno's men were collected, boxed, and loaded onto the steamer. During the afternoon, a small boat of merchants arrived at the camp and began selling their wares. Straw hats were the hot item.

After dark, Custer called his subordinate officers together. Orders for the march were given. What struck most of the officers was the tone of Custer's speech. For possibly the first time since leaving Fort Abraham Lincoln, they fully understood the seriousness of the situation they would be facing. Later that evening, many troops wrote letters home and some even prepared their wills.

Custer Camp #24

Yellowstone River

Figure 69. Custer Camp #24 as viewed from the Highway 446 bridge west of Rosebud, Montana. (photo location: GPS 46.274404, -106.464833, facing east)

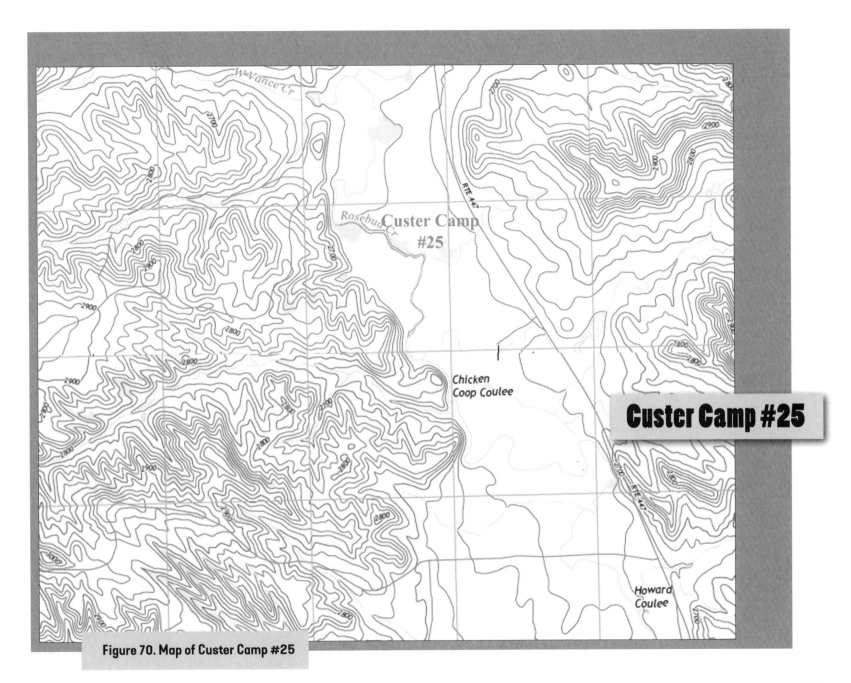

Figure 70. Map of Custer Camp #25

Custer Camp #25

June 22, 1876

General Location: 9.9 miles south of Rosebud, Montana

Ownership Status: private property but visible from public road

GPS Coordinates: 46.132634, -106.462394

Directions:

1. From I-94 West, take Exit 103 to Montana Highway 447 (Rosebud Creek Road).

2. Turn south (left) onto MT 447 and go 9.9 miles. At this point, a small cairn and an interpretive panel will be on the west (right) side of the road.

Well before dawn on June 22, cargo was already being offloaded from the *Far West*. The soldiers of the 7th Cavalry would soon be issued fifteen days' rations for their mission. Each trooper would carry on his horse twelve pounds of oats, one hundred rounds of ammunition for his rifle, and twenty-four rounds of ammo for his pistol. The remaining forage and ammunition would be carried on pack mules. Each company of the regiment had twelve such mules assigned to it.

Custer received his written orders at his tent late in the morning. General Terry was a lawyer before joining the army, and this background was evident in the wording of Custer's orders. They were crafted in such a way that no matter what happened, Terry would be covered. They were so well written, in fact, that historians have been debating the General's intentions ever since. Standard practice in the military, then and now, is to make multiple copies of orders and file them at the various levels of command. Copies of Terry's orders to Custer still exist today.

At noon, Custer and his regiment moved out from the camp on the Yellowstone. They formed into columns of four and passed in review for Terry, Gibbon, and Brisbin. The Regimental Band had been left behind at the Powder River Depot, but the 7th Cavalry's twelve buglers were assembled into a makeshift band to play "Garryowen" as they turned and marched up Rosebud Creek. As Custer bid farewell to Terry, Colonel Gibbon famously said, "Now Custer, don't be greedy, but wait for us!" To which Custer ambiguously replied "No, I will not."

The regiment started up the east bank of Rosebud Creek but soon moved to the opposite side. The course of the Rosebud is especially sinuous and requires frequent fording as the valley is followed upstream. After riding almost twelve miles, the soldiers were back on the east side of the creek when they halted for the night. Officers' call that evening was even more somber than the night before. Custer decreed there would be no more calls by bugle unless absolutely necessary. Lieutenant Godfrey, in his diary, recalled that Lieutenant Wallace said he believed Custer would be killed. Wallace, according to Godfrey, claimed he had never heard the General "talk as he did, or his manner so subdued."

Custer's twenty-fifth campsite was one of the earliest of his camps to be marked. A cairn was placed along the road in the early twentieth century, but no record remains of who placed it or exactly when. A modern placard was added to the site in 2017 by the Community Foundation of Northern Rosebud County.

Custer Camp
#25

GEN. CUSTER
CAMPED HERE
JUNE 22, 1876

Figure 71. Custer's twenty-fifth campsite, his first as he traveled up Rosebud Creek, has been marked for many years. (photo location: GPS 46.133470, 106.460683, facing west)

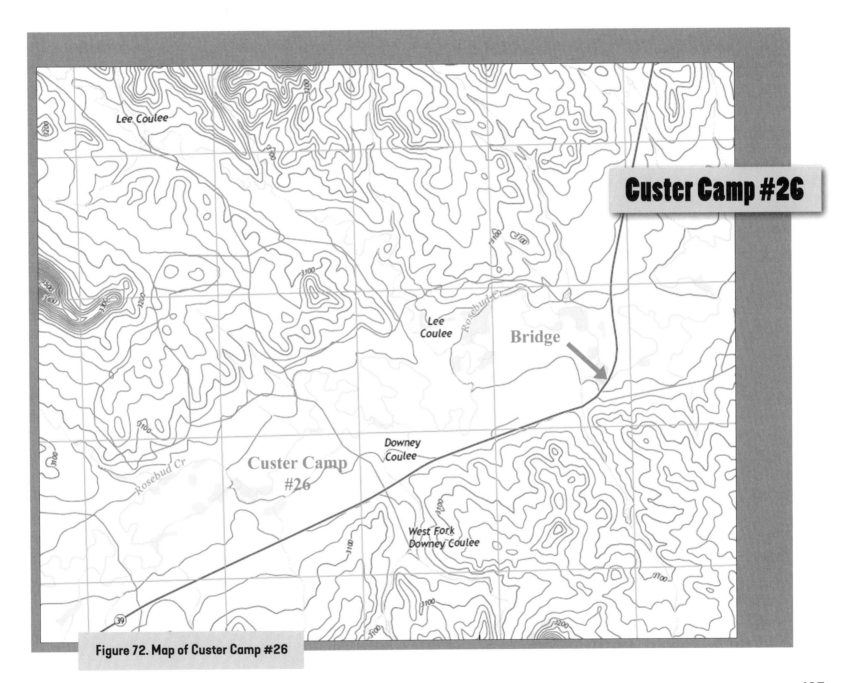

Custer Camp #26

Lee Coulee

Lee
Coulee

Rosebud Cr

Bridge

**Custer Camp
#26**

Downey
Coulee

Rosebud Cr

West Fork
Downey Coulee

39

Figure 72. Map of Custer Camp #26

Custer Camp #26

June 23, 1876

General Location: 8.6 miles south of Colstrip, Montana

Ownership Status: private property but visible from public road

GPS Coordinates: 45.760727, -106.600084

Directions:

1. From Custer Camp #25, continue south on Montana Highway 447 for 31.3 miles until it intersects Montana Highway 39. Note that approximately six miles south of Custer Camp #25, MT 447 becomes a gravel road.

   OR

1. From the town of Colstrip, head south on Montana Highway 39 for 9.3 miles to the intersection of MT 39 and MT 447.

2. From the intersection of MT 39 and MT 447 (Rosebud Creek Road), continue west on MT 39 for 1.4 miles. At this point, a cairn and placard will be located on the north (right) side of the highway.

Although Custer had refused to bring the Gatling guns with him, the movement up the valley of the Rosebud was nevertheless slow and tedious. The regiment was still not proficient with the use of pack mules. Soon after leaving the twenty-fifth camp, the column crossed from the east to the west side of Rosebud Creek again. The train of mules was at the rear of the march, and with each stream crossing they fell further and further behind. By the end of the day, the column was several miles long.

Early in the day's march, the remains of a recent Indian camp were discovered. It was estimated that perhaps four hundred tepees once occupied the site. As they moved further up the valley, more camps and signs of recent Indian activity were found. The regiment traveled thirty-three miles before halting. Again, they found themselves camping on the east side of Rosebud Creek.

Custer Camp #26

Figure 73. Custer Camp #26. The original cairn was placed here early in the twentieth century, and the interpretive panel was added in 2017 by the Custer Circle Project of the Rosebud County Pioneer Museum. (photo location: GPS 45.757438, -106.599814, facing north)

Figure 74. Deer Medicine Rocks are located between Custer Camps #26 and #27 along Rosebud Creek. The sites are sacred to the Northern Cheyenne and Sioux, so the exact location is not given in this book. It was near this landmark that a Sun Dance ceremony was conducted and Sitting Bull had his vision of soldiers falling into the Indians' camp.

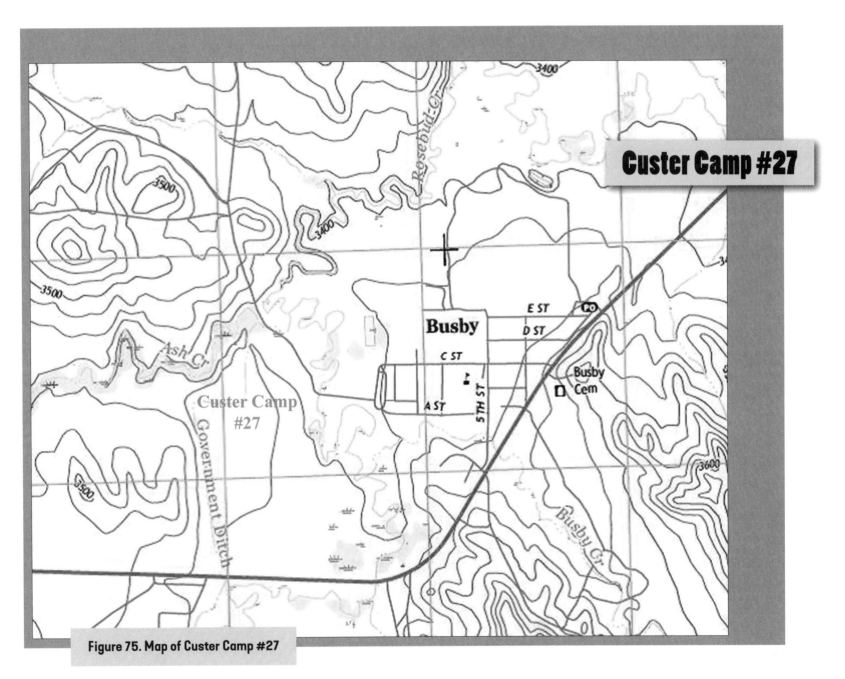

Custer Camp #27

Figure 75. Map of Custer Camp #27

Custer Camp #27

June 24, 1876

General Location: west edge of Busby, Montana

Ownership Status: private property but visible from public road

GPS Coordinates: 45.535498, -106.969843

Directions:

The town of Busby can be approached from the east or the west along US Highway 212.

There is often some confusion regarding the actual location of Custer's campsite at Busby. Evan S. Connell's book *Son of the Morning Star* is a classic and is considered by many to be the definitive account of the Battle of the Little Bighorn. In his book, Connell said the Busby Post Office marked the location of Custer's camp; the post office Connell wrote about was on the west side of Busby. That office burned down years ago and was replaced by a new one on the east side of town.

Soon after breaking camp and resuming the march on June 24, Custer came to a large, abandoned Indian camp. As it turned out, this was the site of Sitting Bull's Sun Dance two weeks earlier. During that ceremony, Sitting Bull had his famous vision of soldiers falling headfirst into the Lakota camp. Above the camp towered Deer Medicine Rocks. This landmark was and still is sacred to the Northern Cheyenne. The Lakota had learned of the site's medicine long before the 1876 battle. In 2012, Deer Medicine Rocks was designated a National Historic Landmark. Because of its spiritual and cultural importance to the Northern Cheyenne, the exact location of Deer Medicine Rocks has been redacted from the supporting federal documents. Likewise, the GPS coordinates are not included in this book. However, the monument is located within sight of Montana Highway 447 between Custer's twenty-sixth camp and the town of Lame Deer.

While examining the frame of the Sun Dance lodge, Custer called his officers together. As the meeting was taking place, Custer's guidon fell over in the breeze. Lieutenant Godfrey, standing nearby, picked up the flag and stuck it into the ground. It fell over a second time, and again he picked it up. He claimed it did not impress him at the time, but another officer later told Godfrey the falling flag was regarded by many as a sign of bad things to come.

Around sundown, camp was established along Rosebud Creek at the present town of Busby. The column had marched twenty-eight miles. The Indian scouts were still somewhere ahead on the trail when the troops bedded down for the night. At 9:00 p.m. some of the scouts came into camp and said they believed a large Indian camp was located in the nearby valley west of the Wolf Mountains. Custer sent Lieutenant Varnum back with the scouts to verify what they had reported. He then ordered the rest of the regiment to be ready to move at 11:00 p.m. It was a short night after a long day's ride. For George Armstrong Custer and many of his followers, the twenty-seventh camp of the expedition would be their last.

Custer Camp #27

Figure 76. Custer's twenty-seventh and final camp was located along Rosebud Creek on the western edge of present-day Busby, Montana. (photo location: GPS 45.528431, -106.962962, facing north from the Highway 212 bridge over Rosebud Creek)

Afterword

In the Introduction, I stated my plans not to delve into Custer's character or the tactics of the battle. I cannot, however, simply leave readers in Busby, Montana, so very briefly, here is what happened next.

At approximately 11:00 p.m. on the evening of June 24, 1876, the 7th Cavalry resumed its march up Rosebud Creek. Less than two miles upstream from Busby, Davis Creek joins the Rosebud from the southwest. The soldiers turned and followed Davis Creek another ten miles until they reached a concealed area just east of the Crow's Nest (GPS 45.446838, -107.139911). The Crow's Nest was a point on a ridge above a small cove from which the valley of the Little Bighorn could be seen. At about 2:00 a.m. the column halted. Custer planned to stay here and rest his troops and horses for the day. As daylight arrived on June 25, Custer's scouts saw what they believed to be evidence of a vast encampment ahead in the valley of the Little Bighorn River. Through the smoke in the valley, the scouts were confident they saw a large herd of horses. Custer tried in vain to see the horses and the camp; he never did. Mitch Boyer, one of Custer's scouts, assured him, "If you don't find more Indians in that valley than you ever saw together before, you can hang me."[18]

During the overnight march from their camp near Busby, one of the pack mules lost a box of supplies. When soldiers went back for the cargo, they discovered the box had already been found by Indians. The soldiers reported this, and Custer assumed the regiment had been spotted. He believed he had lost the element of surprise.

By late morning, the 7th Cavalry was on the march again. They crossed the Wolf Mountains at a natural pass called The Divide (GPS 45.457103, -107.149679). The regiment then started down the valley of a stream now referred to as Reno Creek. Beyond this point, all of Custer's decisions, as well as the tactical maneuvering of his subordinate commands, have been analyzed and re-analyzed by generations of historians. In all likelihood you, the reader, have already formed opinions based upon many retellings of the story. It is my hope that after following Custer's path from Fort Abraham Lincoln, your appreciation for the events leading up to and into the battle has been, or will be, enhanced.

---

[18]Joan Nabseth Stevenson, *Deliverance from the Little Bighorn: Doctor Henry Porter and Custer's Seventh Cavalry* (Norman: University of Oklahoma Press, 2012).

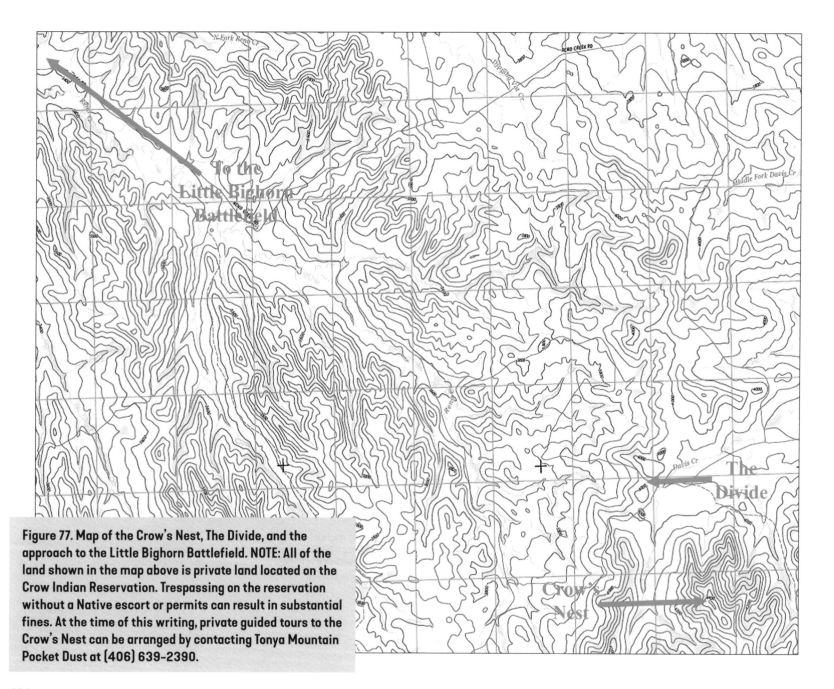

Figure 77. Map of the Crow's Nest, The Divide, and the approach to the Little Bighorn Battlefield. NOTE: All of the land shown in the map above is private land located on the Crow Indian Reservation. Trespassing on the reservation without a Native escort or permits can result in substantial fines. At the time of this writing, private guided tours to the Crow's Nest can be arranged by contacting Tonya Mountain Pocket Dust at (406) 639-2390.

Appendix

USGS Topographic Maps Used in this Guide

Campsite	Map Name	County	State
1	Crown Butte Lake	Morton	ND
2	Sweet Briar	Morton	ND
3	New Salem	Morton	ND
4	North Almont	Morton	ND
5	Glen Ullin NE	Morton	ND
6	Hebron	Stark	ND
7[19]	Antelope	Stark	ND
	Richardton SE	Stark	ND
	Richardton	Stark	ND
	Indian Butte	Stark	ND
8	Boyle	Stark	ND
9	New Hradac South	Stark	ND
10	Belfield SW	Stark	ND
11	Fryburg	Billings	ND
12	Tracy Mountain	Billings	ND
13	Chimney Butte	Billings	ND
14	Buffalo Gap Campground	Golden Valley	ND

Campsite	Map Name	County	State
15[20]	Wibaux	Wibaux	MT
	Red Top Butte	Wibaux	MT
16	Carlyle NW	Wibaux	MT
17	Baker NE	Fallon	MT
18[21]	Ismay North	Custer	MT
	Ismay South	Custer	MT
19	Locate	Custer	MT
20[22]	Calypso	Prairie	MT
	Zero	Prairie	MT
21	Kinsey	Custer	MT
22 a & b	Miles City	Custer	MT
23	Hathaway	Rosebud	MT
24	Rosebud	Rosebud	MT
25	Rosebud Buttes	Rosebud	MT
26	Colstrip	Rosebud	MT
27	Busby	Bighorn	
Crow's Nest	Thompson Creek NW	Bighorn	MT

[19]Campsite #7 is located at the common corner of these four maps.

[20]Camp #15 was located along the common edge of these two maps.
[21]Camp #18 was located along the common edge of these two maps.
[22]Camp #20 was located along the common edge of these two maps.

Bibliography

Anders, Frank L. *The Custer Trail: A Narrative of the Line of March of Troops Serving in the Department of Dakota in the Campaign Against Hostile Sioux, 1876, Fort Abraham Lincoln to the Montana Line.* Edited by John M. Carroll. Glendale: The Arthur H. Clark Company, 1983.

Bell, Gordon and Beth L. "General Custer in North Dakota," *North Dakota History: Journal of the Northern Plains* 31, no. 2 (1964).

Burdick, Usher L. and Eugene D. Hart. *Jacob Horner and the Indian Campaigns of 1876 and 1877: The Sioux and Nez Perce.* Baltimore: Wirth Brothers, 1942.

Chandler, Zachariah. Letter to William Belknap, February 1, 1866. National Archives, 1875 - File No. 6160 (Chandler, Z - District of Columbia). https://catalog.archives.gov/id/142952918. Last accessed September 8, 2019.

Chorne, Laudie J. *Following the Custer Trail of 1876,* 3rd ed. Edited by Sheila Hinkel. Bismarck: Trails West, 1997.

Custer, Elizabeth B. *"Boots and Saddles" or Life in Dakota with General Custer.* London: American Cowboy Books, 2015. Kindle.

Godfrey, Edward Settle. *The Godfrey Diary of the Battle of the Little Bighorn.* Big Byte Books, Kindle Edition 2014.

Kellogg, Mark H. Diary, 1876. Item 20017, State Archives and Historical Research Library, State Historical Society of North Dakota. Available at https://www.history.nd.gov/archives/Kelloggdiary.pdf

Libby, Orin G. *The Arikara Narrative of the Campaign Against the Hostile Dakotas,* June 1876. Bismarck: State Historical Society, 1920.

National Park Service. Visitor Use Statistics. https://irma.nps.gov/Stats/. Last accessed September 8, 2019.

Scott, Douglas D. et al. *Archeological Perspectives on the Battle of the Little Bighorn.* Norman: University of Oklahoma Press, 1989.

Stevenson, Joan Nabseth. *Deliverance from the Little Bighorn: Doctor Henry Porter and Custer's Seventh Cavalry.* Norman: University of Oklahoma Press, 2012.

Terry, Alfred Howe. *The Terry Diary: Battle of the Little Bighorn.* Bellevue, WA: Big Byte books. Kindle Edition 2014.

US Forest Service, History and Culture of the Dakota Prairie Grasslands, https://www.fs.usda.gov/main/dpg/learning/history-culture, last accessed September 16, 2019.

Utley, Robert M. Foreword to *Custer, the Seventh Cavalry, and the Little Big Horn: A Bibliography.* Edited by Michael O'Keefe. Glendale: Arthur H. Clark Company, 2012.

Works Progress Administration. *North Dakota, A Guide to the Northern Prairie State.* Bismarck: State Historical Society, 2014.

Index

About the Author

The author's interest in Custer and the Battle of the Little Bighorn began in high school in the late 1970s. As an assignment in his American History class, he and several other classmates had to write and perform a skit about the battle. The seed was planted, but it wasn't until ten years later, after reading *Son of the Morning Star*, by Evans S. Connell, that the roots finally took hold. He has read numerous books on the subject since that time, and he has visited the battlefield on three separate occasions.

Don Weinell's formal education is not in history, but rather in biology. In 1982 he graduated from Northeast Louisiana University with a Bachelor of Arts Degree in General Studies, minoring in Biology and Military Science. Upon receiving his degree, he was also commissioned as a Second Lieutenant in the US Army. After serving three years on active duty, he returned to graduate school and earned his Master's of Science Degree in Biology. He continued to serve in the Louisiana Army National Guard and was eventually promoted to Captain.

In 1991, soon after the birth of his first son, he began an almost thirty-year career as an environmental scientist with the Louisiana Department of Environmental Quality. In 1996, three years after the birth of his second son, he resigned his army commission in order to spend more time with his family and his civilian career. As an environmental scientist, Don was involved with various aspects of assessing, monitoring, and regulating the quality of the waters of Louisiana. He also responded to emergencies such as Hurricane Katrina in 2005 and the Deepwater Horizon oil spill of 2010.

After the attacks of September 11, 2001, Don decided to put on a military uniform again. Because of his age, he could not be re-commissioned into the army, so he enlisted in the US Air Force Reserve and was trained as an aircraft mechanic.

In the following years, he continued along two career paths: environmental scientist and aircraft mechanic. During a deployment to Southwest Asia in 2009, he became interested in Oregon Trail history after reading *Massacre along the Medicine Road: A Social History of the Indian War of 1864 in Nebraska Territory*, by Ronald Becher. In 2012, Don began a solo, unsupported bicycle trip, which followed the original route of the Oregon Trail from Independence, Missouri, to Oregon City, Oregon. This journey became the basis for his first book, *Bicycling the Oregon Trail*, which was released by Caxton Press in 2017.

Building upon that adventure, he and his friend Kevin Nee decided to bicycle the route Custer took leading up to his fateful battle at the Little Bighorn. As they prepared for the ride, Don discovered how little information was readily available about Custer's route. After the journey was completed in 2018, Don decided a better guide to Custer's route was needed. Hence, this book was written.

Don retired from the Air Force Reserves in 2015, and in 2019 he retired from his state environmental scientist position. He currently resides with his wife of thirty-four years, Kate, in Gonzales, Louisiana.

About the Press

North Dakota State University Press (NDSU Press) exists to stimulate and coordinate interdisciplinary regional scholarship. These regions include the Red River Valley, the state of North Dakota, the plains of North America (comprising both the Great Plains of the United States and the prairies of Canada), and comparable regions of other continents. We publish peer reviewed regional scholarship shaped by national and international events and comparative studies.

Neither topic nor discipline limits the scope of NDSU Press publications. We consider manuscripts in any field of learning. We define our scope, however, by a regional focus in accord with the press's mission. Generally, works published by NDSU Press address regional life directly, as the subject of study. Such works contribute to scholarly knowledge of region (that is, discovery of new knowledge) or to public consciousness of region (that is, dissemination of information, or interpretation of regional experience). Where regions abroad are treated, either for comparison or because of ties to those North American regions of primary concern to the press, the linkages are made plain. For nearly three-quarters of a century, NDSU Press has published substantial trade books, but the line of publications is not limited to that genre. We also publish textbooks (at any level), reference books, anthologies, reprints, papers, proceedings, and monographs. The press also considers works of poetry or fiction, provided they are established regional classics or they promise to assume landmark or reference status for the region. We select biographical or autobiographical works carefully for their prospective contribution to regional knowledge and culture. All publications, in whatever genre, are of such quality and substance as to embellish the imprint of NDSU Press.

We changed our imprint to North Dakota State University Press in January 2016. Prior to that, and since 1950, we published as the North Dakota Institute for Regional Studies Press. We continue to operate under the umbrella of the North Dakota Institute for Regional Studies, located at North Dakota State University.